*Harnessing Heaven* is a fascinating and page-turning story of one man's journey from his ego to his soul. I felt I was being carried on a wave of healing, to the destination of authentic power, profound wisdom, and universal love.
—Dr. Tammi Baliszewski, host of *Journey to Center* on Empower Radio

*Harnessing Heaven* is a first-person account of the fact that there is much more to us than a physical body. Anyone who has ever asked the question, "Surely there is more to life than this?" will find this book a welcome resource!
—Kevin J. Todeschi, Executive Director & CEO
    Edgar Cayce's A.R.E. / Atlantic University
    Edgar Cayce's Association for Research and Enlightenment (A.R.E.)

Clifford Michaels lives and writes through his awakened heart - the heart of love and wisdom that is destined for us all, and that brings God's essence into everyday life through everyday people. The inspired message through his book *Harnessing Heaven* is one that will bring much needed healing to the world.
—Dr. Leslie Wells, Radio Talk Show Host
    The Dr. Leslie Show / Presenter of EVE Consciousness

# HARNESSING HEAVEN

*How One Reluctant
Wall-Streeter Tapped the
Power of the Hereafter*

Introducing Seven Principles for
Clarifying Your Life Purpose

CLIFFORD MICHAELS

Highland Group, LLC
New York

Copyright ©2016 Clifford Michaels
All rights reserved. No part of this book may be reproduced or utilized in any form without permission in writing from the author.

Disclaimer: Clifford Michaels has designed this book to provide information in regard to the subject matters covered. The purpose of this book is to educate. It is sold with the understanding that the author is not liable for the misconception or misuse of information provided. Every effort has been made to make this book as complete and as accurate as possible. The author shall have neither liability nor responsibility to any person or entity with respect to any loss, damage, or injury caused or alleged to be caused directly or indirectly by the information contained in this book.

Published by:
Highland Group LLC, PO Box 1603, New York, NY 10150
www.HarnessingHeaven.com.

Cover design: Kathi Dunn, dunn-design.com
Interior design: Dorie McClelland, springbookdesign.com

Printed in the United States of America
First edition

ISBN: 978-0-9966681-5-6

*With love and gratitude to my family and friends*

## Permissions

Edgar Cayce Foundation
Edgar Cayce's A.R.E.
Association for Research and Enlightenment
215 67th Street
Virginia Beach, VA 23451
www.edgarcayce.org

# Contents

Introduction  ix

## PART 1: A Higher Calling

**Chapter 1.** Never Saw This Coming  5
Benefits of Commuting • Getting Too Comfortable • The Seed Is Planted

**Chapter 2.** Seeking Truth  27
Letting Go • Being Open-Minded

**Chapter 3.** The Circle: A Bridge to Enlightenment  35
Back to School • Stepping Stones • The Enlightenment • Seven Principles for Clarifying Your Life Purpose

## PART 2: Universal Truths

**Chapter 4.** Principle One: Loving Each Other  53
A Lighter Heart • Walking Your Own Line • Keys to Open the Heart • The Time Is Now

**Chapter 5.** Principle Two: Thoughts and Emotions Are "Alive"   65

Releasing the Past • The Aura • Innate Instincts • Shielding the Heart • Emotional Development • False Imprisonment • Internalizing • The Luminous Body • Fear as an Emotion • Evolving beyond Fear to Love and Gratitude

**Chapter 6.** Principle Three: The Power of Unity   91

One Earth, One Voice • The Reality of Our Life • Religion • History Repeats Itself • Politics • Hope Comes with Changing Vibration • Economics • In the Age of Spiritual Advancement • Anyone Can Commune with Heaven • Issues to Contemplate • A New Standard

**Chapter 7.** Principle Four: School Is Never Out   119

Personality versus the Soul • Evolution of Knowledge • Swimming with the Current • Hopelessness Is an Illusion • Personal Lessons • The Earth as a Teacher

## PART 3: EMBRACING YOUR SOUL'S JOURNEY

**Chapter 8.** Principle Five: Creating Is Always in Season   141

Embrace Your Truth • Loving What You Do • The Power of Intention • Life Is a Cocreation

**Chapter 9.** Principle Six: The Orchestra behind the Scenes   153

Angels among Us • Supportive Energy • Coincidences • The Yuwipi Ceremony • Everyone Needs a Coach

**Chapter 10.** Principle Seven: Your Thinking Equals Your Experience   167

Control Your Mind, Control Your Life • Framing • Seeking Peace • Global Coming of Age • You Can Decide

*Contents*

# PART 4: IT STARTS WITH YOU

**Chapter 11.** The Journey Within   *187*

Everyone Is an Enlightenment Center • Seven-Step Process for Spiritual Expansion and Healing • Tuning In to Your Higher Self • Methods for Raising Your Energy Vibration • A Spiritual Circle: Working with Heaven • Spiritualism • The Journey Continues

**Chapter 12.** Harnessing Heaven   *209*

Syncing with Nature • Transformation • You Are a Big Spirit • You Were Born to Rise

Acknowledgments   *223*

Appendix A: Chakra Energy Centers (illustration)   *225*

Appendix B: Evaluating Your Energy Centers to Raise Your Vibration   *228*

Appendix C: Resources for Learning about Energy and Spirituality   *234*

Notes   *239*

About the Author   *245*

# Introduction

I have long been curious about the meaning of life and why we are here, as well as what happens when our life ends and whether there is an afterlife—if, as science tells us, energy is neither created nor destroyed, where does it go? Yet many people throughout history have *feared* death because they have been taught there is retribution in a heaven and a hell, or believe that when we are dead, we cease to exist in any form at all.

Some believe it may be better not to ponder our own mortality to protect our sanity. Ironically, the reverse is true. In the insanity of today's fast-paced and war-torn world, it is enlightening to know who we really are. It is beneficial to understand what occurs when our body gives out and we cross over to the nonphysical dimensions of reality. We might act differently if we knew there was a higher intelligence around us and that our actions in life had consequences beyond our current existence.

Through an unplanned path my life took, I discovered answers to these very questions about life and death, and this has significantly changed my perspectives and attitudes about my existence here. Like perhaps many of you, I had no extraordinary abilities and no religious gospel, yet I awakened to the point of being able to glimpse what awaits us after this life, thereby providing more meaning to what each of us does with this lifetime. By sharing in my experiences, you may better understand the answers to your own questions and come to know that you have nothing to fear—in either life or death—and that in fact you have a much-needed contribution to make to this world.

Life is a learning process, and lessons are often placed in our path whether we are ready for them or not. The benefit of overcoming these challenges is the enlightenment we absorb when the full experience is behind us as a memory. Undergoing a life-threatening illness while working on Wall Street, I discovered the hard way that while humanity has evolved in technology, there is a great need to catch up in the areas of spirituality, compassion, empathy, sympathy, and addressing the needs of our fellow humans.

In our fast paced lives, little of this comes into mind while we are too busy to consider our choices. Often it is a shock, such as a life-threatening illness, as in my case, the death of a friend or relative, or even a huge disappointment in our life, that forces us to become still enough for reflection.

Quieting our mind for that brief moment of reflection can lead to inspiration and is something for which many do not make time. Some of us may not know how to find that still place. We are usually too busy responding to the next urgent call that pops up or checking something off our "to do" list. And, understandably, there is often a sense of accomplishment when we check something off our list or successfully put out the next fire before it starts.

We all have dreams and visions when we are young and unburdened, only to put them aside in favor of day-to-day "grown-up" activities. Some are unable to handle the stress of responsibilities and turn to distractions such as alcohol, drugs, food, or spending to reduce the pressure. If we get caught up in making money, we may not take the time to follow an instinct calling us to pursue other ideals. Despite having varying degrees

*Introduction*

of success in our lives, real progress often seems slow and inconsistent—and far less satisfying than we had hoped.

However, I am here to tell you that there *is* hope! A growing number of people understand that there are other dimensions that exist beyond our normal senses and that we are multidimensional beings capable of great things. This book chronicles my journey into the world of the spiritual unknown and the resultant deepening of these qualities within myself. It is greatly inspired by a higher Source, with wisdom and inspirational messages. There is no tap dancing around the issues; I present to you exactly what I experienced, though it may seem a stretch to some. I invite you to have a discerning mind as you read the information as it may apply to your own life. Allow the written words to sit and find their place within your own being; allow inspiration to follow in whatever creative sparks are ignited in you.

The writing in the pages that follow contains not only my personal story of healing, transformation, and learning about and interacting with these other dimensions, but also information that is vital for all of us to progress if the world intends on surviving and thriving for centuries to come. There are practical exercises for spiritual awakening and expansion, including meditations and the activation of energy centers, as well as methods to achieve optimal health for your body, mind, heart, and spirit.

There are a few things you should know about me: I am an independent thinker and not easily led, making me a natural skeptic. In high school, I received a nearly perfect score on the New York State geometry regent's exam, which was higher than that of all of my classmates who went on to Ivy League schools. My analytic ability and rational thinking mind provide a good measuring stick for observation. My communication skills from business are strong; I am self-made, very curious, and have an open mind for exploration and research. And yet as one not innately open and receptive to the events and learnings I share with you here, I have had experiences that have opened the doors to a new way of perceiving the universe and our place in it. I am convinced that this is possible for *you* as well.

The wonderment of this all is I was the last person anyone would have expected to heal on all these levels through this work. I am no different from anyone else, with the possible exception of being naturally more curious. I know that if I could do this type of transformational work, so can every other person. In our deepest essence, we are all much more alike than we are different.

It is important to note that this information comes not only from my heart, mind, and experiences, but also from collaboration with divine influences in the nonphysical realms of existence. I am one of many messengers willing to share these important teachings, and you will find this wisdom sprinkled throughout the book, set in italics and preceded and followed with a special symbol (࿎). Please pay special attention when you see these specific communications from heaven, also referred to here as "the other side," "beyond the veil," or the "spiritual dimension."

It is time for this knowledge that has been in the hands of a few to be in the hands of the many. I invite you to join me on our common evolutionary journey, with the ultimate goal of bringing the people of our planet closer together—away from separation, conflict, and disharmony, and toward interconnectedness, peace, service, and love.

My wish for you is that after reading this book, you will have a better understanding of who you are, why you are here, and where you fit in the cycle of life. I hope it is a valuable tool for you and others, and that it can inspire people to make positive changes and contributions that could have a beneficial ripple effect around the world.

*With love, faith and inspiration,*
*Clifford Michaels*

# Harnessing Heaven

PART ONE

# A Higher Calling

*If you're right and you know it, speak your mind.
Even if you are the minority of one, the truth is still the truth.*
—Gandhi, goodreads.com

CHAPTER 1

# Never Saw This Coming

*It isn't until you come to a spiritual understanding of who you are—not necessarily a religious feeling, but deep down, the spirit within—that you can begin to take control.*

—Oprah Winfrey, izquotes.com

As a kid out of school, it was awe inspiring when I stood on Wall Street for the first time facing the New York Stock Exchange. It was a beautiful day in the summer of 1982 as I looked upon the skyscrapers that surrounded me. As I glanced west, there was the famous Trinity Church with the World Trade Center in the background, and as I looked east, you could see the East River. It was just magnificent.

I was so excited on the way to my first job interview. Little did I realize how naive I was and that the economic recession at that time was going to create a high hurdle for me. This interview was only the first of many that would continue for five months before several job offers rolled in by January 1983.

I dreamed of making it big and figured everyone who works on Wall Street is rich. At least that is the perception, but the reality is different. Those at the top are well compensated; otherwise, at that time there was an "old boy" network determining who got the best opportunities, and who you knew usually was the key ingredient.

Although I earned enough money to buy an apartment and make some investments, after ten years I was far from rich and already nursing an ulcer from the daily stresses. In my first job, I had been thrown right onto a trading desk where my responsibility was enormous, trading millions of dollars of securities. There were others watching over me as a backstop to any significant trading errors, but that sometimes added to the pressure as well. Furthermore, in addition to the standard office politics, there were a number of office romances in this small firm of seventy-five people—the managing director, for one, had an actress/model twenty years his junior following him around. Not an ideal example for us junior traders to aspire to, as it showed he was less interested in managing money than in his extracurricular activities; who could believe anything he would say? And then came word that the owner of the firm was being investigated by the IRS, as the whole business operation was nothing more than a tax shelter for him. It wasn't long before I needed to find somewhere else to work, and a dose of reality set in that I was no longer in the safety of school or family. This was the real world of political maneuvering—every person for him- or herself and a dog-eat-dog mentality.

In a ten-year period, I worked for four Wall Street firms and had eleven bosses. It was a merry-go-round as companies opened and closed their doors, merged, or expanded depending on who was in charge. Sometimes, whole units of people would just pick up and leave to go to another firm offering a sweeter deal. It was a transient business with no loyalties, to say the least, and I was part of it.

Disillusionment eventually set in, especially after witnessing men more successful and older than I was, with families to support, get pink slips because the company found a way to do the business more profitably. They were asking younger people like me to do the same work for less cost, disregarding the years of hard work and sacrifice others had made to the firm. I found myself thinking, *What happens when I'm older and earning more money? Do I become vulnerable to younger people?* Though I might have been temporarily part of the "solution" for the company, I was also contributing to the new "problem" for those whose slots I filled. As time went on, this troubled me more and more. Added to this I started to wonder, *What am I doing anyway to help others as I'm looking at numbers on a screen each day? Am I making a difference to anyone?*

Being a trading warrior is not glamorous, and often I was defined by how well I outsmarted another trader I did not know. If I made money it felt good, but if I lost money it was a lousy feeling and I became hard on myself. A lot of negative self-talk and mentally kicking myself usually followed if I was on a losing streak. After a while, I felt that none of this mattered in the long run and that it was detrimental to define myself this way. Yet so many Wall Street traders do define themselves in this manner, and it can lead to terrible consequences, from drug addictions and alcoholism to suicide; I did not want this to happen to me. While negotiating the challenges of global markets moving up, down, and sideways from hour to hour was invigorating and provided an adrenaline rush; even the money I earned could no longer replace the growing emptiness inside me each day.

After accumulating a good amount of financial capital by the time I was thirty, I decided to start my own financial planning firm and bring my knowledge directly to individuals and private businesses. My motivation for leaving corporate America and starting my own practice was to make a difference, be a trusted adviser, and help people get their financial house in order. Though I was not especially religious and not practicing any formal religion, I was hoping that if there was a higher power that cared, it would support me in being successful.

Four years into the new business with most of my savings depleted, I began questioning my faith and asking why this was happening to me. After all, hadn't I done many of the right things in life, and weren't my intentions good?

Hiding under my school desk in case of nuclear war as a kid and seeing people kill each other on the world news each night as an adult had served as an impetus for me to search for a higher power. Even though I did not have a strong belief system in God, I had attended synagogue and religious school as a youth, which provided some framework to speak to the Creator, though the focus of school seemed more about the history of the Middle East than anything else. The truth was that I relied more on myself than on others, as some people had let me down at one time or another and so, I believed, had God, since I never felt as if my prayers were being answered.

What's more, I could not truly understand the Creator no matter what someone else had to say. And there were so many different opinions about this Supreme Being, which was referred to by many different names in different religious and spiritual paths—what it was and what it stood for. It seemed that all one had to do was turn on the television set any Sunday morning and find out whatever one needed to know—sort of. Each station had a different preacher, and a couple of them were even in the tabloids in a scandal or two. I did not know what to think anymore. One thing that was becoming clearer to me, though, was that with so many faiths all claiming to be the right path to God, there had to be some universal current that could tie them all together. Otherwise, religion and the way people defined themselves as different from each other was to me an exercise in insanity.

However, my questions around Spirit and its involvement in my personal life gradually retreated again, as I came to fully understand that building a business from scratch was challenging and needed all my attention. Eventually, though, with perseverance and relying on my intuition, things began to fall into place.

While living in New York City at age thirty-nine as a newlywed, I felt my life seemed to have so much promise until one morning when I "just happened" to be late for work to my office, which was three blocks down from the World Trade Center. As I was dressing, I noticed something on TV: the tail end of a plane sticking out from a large building while the rest of it was burning inside one of the Twin Towers. It was September 11, 2001.

I had lived through the first bombing of the World Trade Center in 1994, and my awareness was on high alert for acts of terrorism. Back then, I was working directly across the street from Tower One and the Vista Hotel, where the first attack occurred. When the bomb went off, my office shook as if one of the New York City harbor helicopters had struck it. When my office coworkers and I exited the building, I was in awe looking at the miles of emergency vehicles that lined the West Side Highway for as far as my eyes could see. It was surreal, and I'll never forget it. At the time, I couldn't imagine this event repeating itself.

Now, sitting on the edge of my bed in 2001, watching in utter disbelief, I witnessed a second plane strike the Twin Towers. Thinking of all the innocent people who might be dead in these buildings and the airplanes was really making me question my faith in a higher power. I was starting to think and feel what it might have been like for people during other wars in history. Shocked to find my own neighborhood under attack, I realized that if there had been any innocence about myself left from childhood, it was lost the morning of 9/11. I had friends, old business associates, and friends of friends who died that day.

Caught up as I was in the preposterous events unfolding before my eyes, suddenly it dawned on me that my own wife, Heather, was working directly across the street from this horrible disaster, and I became frightened for her safety. Sitting in our apartment as the day went on without much communication about what was really going on in the area, as both cell phones and landlines were down, added to my fears. I wondered, *What if she is dead?* And then, *How can I be even thinking these horrible thoughts?* It was unimaginable!

Finally, after an interminable wait of twelve hours, there was a knock at the door. I opened it and there was Heather! She was visibly upset and covered from head to toe in black ash. Relief flooding through me, I hugged her and asked and exclaimed at the same time, "Honey, you're ok?!" Shaking, she replied, "It is a war zone downtown. Everyone and everything is covered in ashes. There is no public transportation, so many of us walked home long distances—even across bridges—to the outer boroughs." Then she pointed to her bare feet, which had just transported her more than 120 city blocks to safety. They were tattered and black and blistered.

Heather explained to me that she had watched the second plane hit with her own eyes. She and a few coworkers were told to stay where they were until authorities gave the all-clear sign, which they never did. They remained huddled for hours in the basement of her office building as the world around them was crumbling to the ground. Eventually, she found the courage to go aboveground and fought her way home through the smoke and devastation that had taken place.

After my wife had finished her story, my attention returned to the terrorists and the families who had lost loved ones. Realizing that the plane crashes had been no accident, I wondered whether my questioning of a higher power in this situation could be similar to other people's thoughts questioning about the existence of God during other wars in history. These questions were too big for me to answer in the moment, but there was one thing I knew for sure: Heather's and my perception of security, as well as that of many of the American people, had just been shattered.

I continued working a few blocks from what was left of the World Trade Center, but something had changed in me. I was not sure what safe and secure meant for me now and needed some time for reflection. When coming up from the underground subway to my building, I was struck by the odor of smoldering ashes. The smell made me emotionally sick and depressed over the loss of life and was a reminder that while I had watched the events unfold from my New York City apartment, had I been on time that day I could have easily been right in front of Two World Trade Center when the planes struck. I often had taken the subway just at that time and had been in and out of the World Trade Center for morning meetings.

With these fearful memories firmly in place, it was no wonder Heather and I decided to move away from the area. Like other people who had lived through what became referred to as "9/11" in New York City, we soon began looking for a house in the suburbs. Though I didn't really realize it at the moment, a new phase of my life was about to begin that would include many new life lessons.

Our first home was forty-five miles west of New York, and while the train to work proved challenging, it provided me with time to read and some much-appreciated peace from daily distractions. Despite being the city slicker I was, having lived and worked in New York City for seventeen years, I found that it felt good to own a piece of property and call it home. I was glad to be away from the city, but realized to my dismay that my own heart had become hardened from 9/11, early financial struggles, and even several emotional disappointments in my love life previous to marrying and settling down in the suburbs. The nagging questions about why cruel things happen resurfaced, but I never really got answers that I could understand, and they died down once again.

I immersed myself in our new life outside of the city. The house we had purchased needed a lot of fixing up, as we had bought it below market value. Suddenly, I had to become a handy man and develop a new skill set—I didn't know any city slickers who were really good at fixing things. A few professionals helped us with tile and carpentry, and we took on ourselves a lot of the tasks required to create a home.

As I painted the inside of the house, working with color and design had an interesting effect on me—I felt energized and was surprised by this. I wondered how I was able to do something well that was clearly outside of my educational background and for which I had no experience or training. In contrast to being a *learned* skill, it felt as if this was a natural talent that was coming from another place within myself, one with which I was not very familiar. I liked this newly discovered aspect of my nature!

Another project required that I rent a jack hammer from Home Depot—I thought I could save money in tile removal by trying to jack hammer the front hallway. By chance, my father walked through the front door just as I was flying up and down on this ridiculous piece of equipment. I was using it as a pogo stick, and dust was flying everywhere. As this scene caught him by surprise, he began yelling to get the heck off the jack hammer! Dad insisted on taking cash from his pocket to pay the tile installer to do the tile removal and began reminding me about what was important in life. I suddenly remembered and appreciated the value of parents and their guidance at particular moments in life.

A rewarding feature of our new home was the natural environment that surrounded us. There were woods at the end of the property containing a variety of animals, as well as a man-made pond stocked with goldfish, which I began watching from the back of my porch. I underestimated what this would mean to me until I realized that no matter how difficult a day I had had, if I came home early to sit on the porch, I slowly unwound and melted into the landscape of fish, deer, groundhogs, birds, bees, and other natural critters. Even in colder weather many of the animals were still around, and the change of seasons was magnificent with the colorful flowers and trees.

Being outdoors grounded me, I discovered. The memories of 9/11 began to fade and the stresses of business to lessen. The process of being more involved in the natural world around me began to soften some of what had become hard within.

A year after moving to the suburbs we had our first child, a boy. Oddly, we had tried for two years to get pregnant, and this had included working with top fertility doctors with no success. Then we went on a cruise to France, and during a day excursion, we found ourselves in the basement of a church in the old town of Saint-Émilion. We learned that, apparently, in the eighth century AD, when a woman could not get pregnant, she would visit the monk Saint Émilion in this church, and he would pray and bless her on a particular stone bench. According to the monks who live there now, many times women blessed this way would then conceive. After hearing this, we sat in the exact location on the stone bench where this ritual had taken place and prayed. To my disbelief, four weeks later Heather was pregnant! Another chapter in my story was unfolding.

The miracle of childbirth is universally awe inspiring. Becoming a first-time father was empowering and a role I took seriously. The responsibility was mine, and the choice had been made freely to bring this child into the world. This was our decision, and as loving parents, we would do everything to give this child an opportunity to succeed.

As any parent knows, having a baby is a learning experience that starts from day one. We learn about babies and in the process learn about ourselves along the way. Parenting requires patience, tolerance, and compassion, and there is no better way to learn these very important life lessons in a short period of time than having a newborn in your family.

One evening when I was getting ready to put our eight-month-old son to sleep, something marvelous occurred. I stood watching him in his crib as he lay flat on his stomach. Suddenly, he raised himself all the way up on his elbows and picked his head up high to look at me. This was no ordinary gaze, as his eyes were fixed, and it appeared that he looked right through me. I could see intelligence deep within that seemed far older and wiser than that of an eight-month-old. As we continued to look deeper into each other's eyes, I felt the power of this being; it truly startled me. Silently, I found myself asking him, *Who are you, little being? What are you here to teach us?* To this day it is an experience I will never forget, and it was an inspiring moment that rekindled my faith that we might be more than just flesh.

## Benefits of Commuting

Since I no longer lived in New York City, the commute to work averaged 1½ hours each way, totaling three hours per day. With so much time to myself, naturally I did some of my office work on the train. After a while, though, there was only so much work to process, and my mind began to focus on books, particularly nonfiction in the areas of self-improvement.

Eventually, I developed an appetite for reading to pass the commuting time; I enjoyed learning new things, so nonfiction was usually on my reading menu. Much to my surprise, though perhaps in part due to Heather's and my experience in the church in Saint-Émilion and her resulting pregnancy, some books completely out of my previous repertoire began to catch my eye. A man by the name of James Van Praagh had written several, one of which was called *Talking to Heaven*, in which he related messages from the nonphysical planes of existence to people for their healing. To promote his book, Van Praagh gave a lecture in the New York area, which I attended out of curiosity. He connected a few people in the audience with loved ones who had "crossed over," as he put it. He was apparently talking both to the spirit of the deceased and to the audience member who had been left to grieve. I was skeptical, yet the specific information he related and the raw emotional response by a number of audience members receiving this information was too accurate to have been orchestrated. It certainly appeared genuine, and this experience stayed with me for quite some time. I was skeptical of life beyond death yet could not deny what I had just witnessed. If nothing else, my curiosity was asking me to learn more.

With three hours of commuting each day, my wife working full time, one young son, and another baby on the way, it was not long before tensions between Heather and me revealed themselves. For example, I worked long hours, so when I was delayed in my commute coming home at night and received a cold shoulder for missing dinner, it stung. Heather, on the other hand, felt she was doing everything. She had to commute to her job while shuffling our son back and forth from day care, as well as preparing a family meal each night—and all this while being pregnant. We both felt unappreciated.

In many ways we were a typical dual-income couple struggling with a work-life balance as we began raising a family. We worked hard for our money and had many expenses to cover as well. It did not take much for tension and stress to make its way into our relationship, and it began taking its toll. We did some marriage counseling and worked through it as best we could as our second child arrived, another boy. We decided to sell our house and move a little closer to New York City for an easier commute.

Our next house did not need as much fixing up as our first, and it provided a more usable backyard for our children to play in without bumping into packs of deer running through our property. It appeared that all our efforts were finally paying off as we established our new home and the pressures eased in our marriage. Life felt good.

## Getting Too Comfortable

I settled into the routines of marriage and family with Heather and our two amazing children, who permitted me the opportunity to be a father. After about seven years, I considered myself fortunate to be where I was in life, both relative to my career and to my personal world. I mistakenly thought I knew what life was all about and that I had it all together.

However, the universe loves change. Being a student of the stock market, I know that everything in life is a cycle and that when investors get too comfortable and overconfident, it usually means the stock market is nearing a turning point—maybe a market top. I had witnessed time and again a stock market make new highs, with investors believing it was easy to make money, only to then see a nasty correction reminding everyone that homework and investment discipline were also needed to succeed. In my personal case, I had gotten comfortable in my life—this was maybe the first time ever that things had seemed this easy—and, sure enough, I began to get one respiratory infection after another. There did not seem to be any logical explanation for it, but with headaches and not much other than antibiotics from doctors, after about a year I decided to visit an allergist in town.

Actually, I had cut myself pulling out weeds, and realized I needed a doctor to remove a piece of the weed that had lodged itself under my skin. While there, I asked for a referral to an allergist. So, it was the landscaping work that led to cutting my hand, which led to this specific doctor. Quite a convoluted sequence of events leading me to a particular allergist who changed my life! Was this more than happenstance, I wondered?

This allergist was an old-timer, not ready for retirement but with plenty of miles under his belt in terms of experience. He did things by the book with a no-nonsense and thorough approach. He suggested a chest x-ray, which revealed spots on one of my lungs. We all feared the worst, including the doctor, as lung cancer became a real concern. I had a CAT scan as a follow-up. I felt completely numb as I entered the narrow machine. My mind tried to dismiss worst-case scenarios, but my dry mouth and beating heart betrayed my panic.

When the results came back, the physician and I had a "good news–bad news" discussion. The good news: the spots on the lung were from an old rib injury that had led to calcification of bone. Wow, I was so relieved—I had dodged a bullet! The bad news: I likely had a malignant growth on my left kidney. This was an incidental finding; *What are the chances of this?* I questioned. Kidney cancer is asymptomatic in its early stages with no pain or way to detect it, which is why it is so lethal.

I had thought the idea was a cliché, but my life really did flash before me. I became panic stricken for my young kids—what if they were left with no father? My eyes began to water up. Further tests revealed I had cancer, and my mind began to race. Initially, my reaction was one of anger—why had this happened just when I thought I had it all? I asked, *Why me? What have I done wrong to deserve this fate early in my life?*

It is difficult to describe how terrified I was the night of the kidney surgery. To say I was forced to reevaluate my life, my choices, and my decisions when faced with the possibility of death is an understatement. A real floodgate opened up that night as I realized that I was not in control of my destiny—and perhaps never had been. This was a time I had to have faith in others besides myself and perhaps faith in a higher power, even though this was normally outside my comfort zone. My life was in the hands of the surgeon and, I came to understand, in the hands of a force I had not spent much time thinking about. That night in intensive care I was panicked and helpless, and I believed I was going to die.

At one point I became even more aware that to the left of me was a man screaming from sickness and pain from extreme high blood pressure, diagonally across the room was a woman with many broken bones trying to defecate in a bed pan and yelling at the top of her lungs, and directly across from me was an old woman being given her last rights from the hospital priest. In the midst of this chaos and fear, I found myself praying to God for help. It was in that moment that time stood still for me, my own pain subsided, and I found peace as I surrendered to a power much greater than myself. Suddenly, the noises in the room subsided, and I heard what I thought was a humming sound or vibration. A greater awareness of my own self took hold, and everything around me was now in slow motion. For those few minutes I did a lot of thinking about my life and what I might do differently if given another chance. Then I fell off into a peaceful sleep. When I awoke a few hours later, against all the nurses' orders for pain management, I insisted they take me off the morphine drip. They stopped the morphine, and, unbelievably, I had little pain.

I thought about my "life purpose," a concept new to me. I had spent so many years trudging along looking only at what was immediately ahead of me and how it might get me to the future I desired that I had not really pondered the point of it all. I learned that night that the lesson we may need is not necessarily something we request; it is often thrust upon us when we least expect it. For me it had resulted in panic, fear, and major distress. I had felt lost, out of control, angry as hell, resentful, and helpless. These were not things I usually allowed myself to feel.

I often had suppressed a lot of my feelings or ignored emotional pain in order to feel better. *This is just how life is,* I'd think to myself—*you hunker down and go on as best you can.* However, when I realized I might be breathing my last breath, I got really determined, desiring a second chance at life. It wasn't until later that I realized this had been an opportunity for soul growth. Ironically, it can be this type of process that moves us forward, not backward, as it might first seem. After all, a kite rises against the wind, not with it. With these new thoughts running through my mind and heart in the midst of this peaceful feeling, I felt an expansion of my own faith. According to the doctors, the surgery had gone well, and I returned home a few days later.

Kidney cancer is curable, *if* caught early, and mine had been in the fifth inning, to use a baseball analogy. If one discovers this illness past the sixth inning, the chance of survival is very slim. This was too close for comfort for me, even though I had survived the surgery and the prognosis was good. With so much responsibility to my family and my clients, I did not have the luxury of sitting back after surgery to see what might happen next. Most doctors will say after surgery that they "got it all," but this does not guarantee that it is gone forever. I proactively did whatever I could to tilt the odds of survival in my favor so that it would not return.

Actually, I had little choice but to take matters into my own hands. This type of cancer represented three percent of all cancers, and there were only a few doctors who specialized in its treatment. I went on a "Listserv" on the Internet. It's like the old phone party lines, but instead it is an e-mail list that anyone around the world can see when joining. People share their knowledge and experiences regarding their disease as more people join in to ask questions about their cancer. It is a powerful way to share information and benefit from others' experiences. It helped me seek out the right medical experts for my particular treatment.

I did research and found out that this form of cancer is "slow growing," so I would have a number of years before it might take my life. It was more than enough time for other business associates, who were a backup for me, to step forward and help, if the need arose. Furthermore, I hardly missed a day of work except for the week when I had my initial surgery, which was done with a laparoscope for a quick recovery. This seemed practical enough; I could plan for any eventuality, or so I thought. It helped me feel somewhat back in control of my life in spite of the attack on my system and psyche.

### The Seed Is Planted

In attempting to permanently heal myself, I was open to anything that could help tip the odds of survival in my favor. This included diet, vitamins, meditation, cleansing programs, books, and anything else that was reasonable and made sense. It is difficult not to be totally focused when desperate and faced with one's mortality.

My doctors introduced me to a phase III experimental drug from Europe for which I volunteered—it teaches the body's immune system to kill this particular kidney cancer cell. It was high technology, and the side effects of the drug were minimum compared to other chemotherapy cancer drugs. I only needed to leave work a little early once a week to receive the drug and then return to the office the next morning for business as usual.

While recovering from the cancer, I began researching alternative therapies, and one name kept coming up when I was on the Internet: "Edgar Cayce." Curiously, one night while I was watching a history show on TV, part of the program talked about alternative healing, and again there was the mention of a man named Edgar Cayce. This was too much of a synchronicity to ignore, and I began to research more about him.

Cayce (1877–1945), also called the "sleeping prophet," I learned, founded the nonprofit Association for Research and Enlightenment (A.R.E.) in Virginia Beach, Virginia. The association, which still exists today, is based on the more than twenty thousand documented psychic health readings he gave to people while in a trance state. He is considered to be the father of holistic medicine. There are a number of books that document his life and the health readings he provided for two decades, from 1920 to 1940. Cayce was said to give these readings in a complete hypnotic trance, during which he was able to tap into the universal consciousness that surrounds us all and present health remedies to people who traveled far and wide to see him. Many times he charged little or nothing at all, as he felt it was his divine task to help people.

Some people speculated he was connecting with his subconscious mind, while others thought it was an intelligence separate from Cayce that came through with a specific healing remedy for each person. While this was all new to me—and a realm that before my illness I would never have imagined myself delving into—I discovered that I could personally access many of these readings and remedies by Cayce, as they were all documented and could be found in books and on CDs. I set aside my skepticism and decided to explore more about his techniques—after all, my life and, by extension, that of my family were at stake!

What was especially interesting to me was that many of the health remedies Cayce provided were not discovered by modern medicine until some years later. All of the remedies were natural substances or therapies that did not require a doctor's prescription.[1]

I began reading some of this published material and found it reasonable for a number reasons: (1) Many of the remedies prescribed back then, as we know today, have medicinal properties; (2) Cayce charged hardly any money for these readings—he just wanted to help others get better; and (3) I used some of his remedies, and my body was indeed feeling better afterward.

The remedies focused on assisting a person to naturally heal his or her own body through better diet, natural products, bowel eliminations, and deeper sleep, and they even offered some wisdom on how emotions interact with illness. A cure did not always result, but many times, as someone's immune system was strengthened by the treatments, that person could be more apt to heal a number of ailments.

In reading about people feeling better and stronger from some of these natural remedies, I also discovered some unintentional but intriguing pieces of information. Some of the Edgar Cayce documented readings were about people's emotions and how they directly impacted their health. This was particularly fascinating to me given what I had been through. And, I learned how stress, anger, and resentment are stored in the human body and can lead to illness and disease.[2] This information was very specific. I read as much as I could on this subject and how it applied to my circumstances—certainly, I acknowledged, I carried a high level of daily stress, and I began to wonder how this might have been related to the cancer I had experienced.

With my personality, once I find a subject interesting I tend to peel back the layers to educate myself more and more; I admit that I can become obsessive. I learned as much as possible as it related to my own health condition, and I implemented some of his suggestions to increase my odds of survival. Interestingly, many of Cayce's readings suggest that much of illness can be prevented and cured by paying closer attention to our emotional states. Anger, resentment, jealousy, and hate all create far more poisons in the blood than do a poor diet.[3]

I also discovered that a few of the twenty thousand readings alluded to "past lives," future predictions, angels, God, a person's energy field, and other subjects that have a spiritual value and actually satisfied some of my curiosity even just in reading about them. While previously I had had little knowledge or opinion about most of these subjects, being more scientifically oriented and somewhat of a natural skeptic, I figured that if Cayce's health remedies were helping me, perhaps his other subject matter might also have value.

I studied more of his readings on life, love, death, and spirituality, and found my own knowledge on these subjects expanding. My views had not changed a lot, but I was certainly more open at this point to this new realm of information than ever before.

The transformation of one who is rooted in everyday life with routines, responsibilities, family, work, etc., to changing his or her perspective of the world and seeing things from a spiritual frame of reference seldom occurs overnight. At best it is gradual; it takes time and patience. The outer world moves at a fast pace, yet when it comes to permanent inner changes that are meaningful, it can take a long time. The cancer cattle prod was a big motivator for me. In many ways it was a blessing, or I might never have truly looked deeply at my life and where I was headed.

The information that I accumulated while healing myself was profound and became significant enough for me to want to share it with others. Initially, my goal was not to do anything for other people when I started out on my quest for health. However, I learned that the healthier one becomes in body and soul, the more naturally we desire to become part of something greater than ourselves. I have come to understand that, as far as I am concerned, there is no individual purpose that is more important than helping other people. I even started to understand why Edgar Cayce had devoted his life and his talents to healing others. When we let go of anger, resentment, and ego, we make room to be filled up with more positive things, such as love and compassion for others. Then we naturally want to share this love, as it is too powerful to be contained.

If we are aware of ourselves in daily life, there is a lesson in everything, whether it feels good or bad at the time we are going through the experience. We are *all* teachers to each other in one form or another, and this is true regardless of what our standing is in society. If we are open to it, we can learn from a child or a homeless person in the street. Children often don't know how to be anything but direct and honest with their feelings, which is something we all can be inspired to emulate. Teachers come in many forms. When we understand that life is a classroom, we can learn in the midst of it just as easily as we did in our more formal schooling.

Each person who embraces the information that follows will have his or her own unique personal experience with it. Each of us is distinctive, with different life circumstances and our own path to follow. There is no linear progression in how we evolve here on Earth; we all possess unique abilities to share with others.

As for me, my goal with all this new learning remained the same: to acquire information and help so that I could fully recover my own health. I didn't want to die; I wanted to learn and to live my life to the fullest. Most importantly, I did not want my kids growing up without their father.

CHAPTER 2

# Seeking Truth

*All truth passes through three stages. First, it is ridiculed. Second, it is violently opposed. Finally, it is accepted as self-evident.*

—Arthur Schopenhauer, brainyquote.com

Several years before my marriage and my health scare—and my ensuing learning about Edgar Cayce and his work—at one point I randomly picked up a book called *Through Time into Healing*, by Dr. Brian Weiss. A psychiatrist, Dr. Weiss hypnotizes his patients to regress back in time as a way to uncover hidden or forgotten memories. The belief is that hypnotic regression may help cure an emotional problem from the past that may be affecting one today.

Dr. Weiss discovered that some patients regressed beyond childhood allegedly into a past life. This surprised him, and he found it difficult to believe at first. However, it continued to happen again and again, with spectacular results in the ultimate beneficial treatment of patients. He compiled these experiences and wrote a book giving specific examples and explaining how some past-life issues are connected to certain people's present-day problems.[1]

Dr. Weiss recorded a great deal of this material in books and ultimately appeared on national television with such shows as Oprah Winfrey's, discussing his experiences with patients. I found his conclusions thought provoking, but I was cynical, for if this was true, then so was reincarnation. And even if they might possibly be true, I wondered how these past-life happenings could be proved. I was a numbers person, and scientific evidence had always been important to me; finance is concrete. While I enjoyed thinking about Dr. Weiss's work and found it intriguing, I could not accept that it could apply to myself. The thought lingered, though, that if any of this *was* true, then life continued beyond the physical.

My father had always said, "When you're dead, you're dead. That's it." So I had never pushed myself to discover life's answers on death and dying; his seeming certainty about the topic had been enough for me. I had been well indoctrinated even before I left the nest and never really had had any reason to question my father's beliefs. Like many people, I had lived my life with no emphasis or awareness of how my behavior and choices could possibly affect how my future would unfold. But that was then, and this was now, and Weiss's experiences were no longer seeming so far-fetched. Having been through this serious health crisis, I found myself questioning old belief systems and my mind beginning to open up to things I would never previously have imagined.

### *Letting Go*

While recovering from cancer, I detoxified my body by ingesting primarily natural foods and substances. My diet helped me to clear myself physically. At the same time, I seemed to experience an emotional detoxification as well. I was letting go of personal disappointments that had built up over the years, and I was calmer. This was easier for me after facing my own mortality. I had more energy and more gratitude for being alive. It was from this reference point that things for me began to shift.

Most of us have lost a family member or loved one to death or certainly will experience this at some time in our lives. For Heather, this had come relatively early. Her mother had died at forty-two years of age, when she at the time was just a teenager.

Heather had held on to this emotional pain for many years, and it was ever-present—in conversations, happy times, or when she watched a sad movie. It did not take much to stimulate what spiritual teacher Eckhart Tolle refers to as her emotional pain body, resulting in tears streaming down her face. From his descriptions, it seemed to me that her thoughts were in the past—that there was an emotional pain body around her, and she was not living in the now.[2]

As many grief counselors will contend, if someone excessively holds on to grief they must be getting some benefit out of it. To me, it seemed that Heather was holding on to this pain because she was holding tight to the closeness of her mother's memory. She seemed afraid to let go and expressed guilt and regret about not being there as her mother lay on her deathbed—at the time of her mother's death my wife was young and away at school during most of her mother's illness.

I don't think grief has to make sense to anyone other than the bereaved, and I know that no one can force another to heal until the one who holds the emotional pain is ready to release it. This certainly was true for Heather. Many years later and still talking about her pain of her mother's death, there remained a sadness deep in her that refused to go away. However, there must have been a subtle openness in her to letting go of this longtime pattern, as something was about to occur that would begin to shift that.

We had just recently attended the James Van Praagh lecture and had seen firsthand what a medium could do in communicating with those who have departed the physical plane of existence. Coincidently, at this time there was an advertisement that kept appearing in a local paper by a woman who also connected people with loved ones who had died and crossed over into the spiritual realm. *Come on, I thought to myself, what are the chances of this?* I dismissed the newspaper ad many times, thinking that this woman was probably a charlatan.

Eventually, however, it occurred to me that perhaps it might benefit Heather to have a session with her. While I had doubts about whether this woman was capable of what she claimed, at the same time I hoped that she could ease my wife's suffering—too many years had gone by with this sadness gnawing at her heart, and I was running out of ideas for helping to relieve it. Heather herself had no belief in this sort of thing, yet she was open-minded to the possibility that it might be authentic. And, if it was not real, she thought, maybe healing on some level could happen anyway. We decided to see this woman.

We made an appointment for a "gallery reading," where a number of us would sit in a small room together with this spiritual medium. She would spend ten minutes per person connecting and communicating with spirits, usually deceased loved ones. She said there were no guarantees as to who might come through, but we both felt this was still worth a try.

At the gallery reading we were seated upstairs with six other people in what appeared to be this woman's attic. It was a finished, sunlit room that had creaky floors, old wooden chairs, and wall hangings that suggested we were in the company of nonphysical entities. I was amused that it seemed somewhat cliché, like the images in old movies might have portrayed. The medium handed out legal pads for us to take notes for each other, as it seemed that the person receiving the reading often became quite emotional and unable to record his or her own messages. The medium started at one end of the room and proceeded to deliver messages down the row to people one at a time. Each reading lasted just long enough for the individual to try to ascertain the validity of the information. Heather and I were near the end of the row, so I was able to watch and listen intently as she delivered specific information for each person before me. From the expression of amazement and joy on other people's faces, I knew it was going to be interesting when she got to us.

The precision of information conveyed to each person along with the fluid delivery of communication was very impressive. I had arrived with an attitude of disbelief, but the emotional reactions of other people to specific information from and about their deceased loved ones really got my attention. People were sobbing, and my heart began racing as my turn neared. The real test would come when the medium finally reached us.

When Heather's reading began, we held our breath and prayed that it would be okay—and was it ever! As the woman delivered the personal information to her, I could not write fast enough while trying to emotionally connect with what was being said. First the medium said, "I have a woman—it's your mother. She says she died before her time." In a whimper, Heather responded, "Yes," as she was fighting back the tears. Then the medium gave details about our two small children. She said, "I see two boys running up and down the hallways of your house after each other, laughing, and they are close in age." Heather and I looked at each other because we did, in fact, have two boys; the medium was right on both counts. Heather again responded, "Yes," and it brought her a smile. The medium began describing things that had happened at our wedding and the difficulties in our marriage, which perhaps could be dismissed as "lucky guesses." However, the grand finale was a precise description of Heather's deceased mother—what she had looked like, how she had died, and other details that only my wife could have known. It appeared the medium was somehow listening to Heather's mother and receiving all this information. In essence, this was proving the existence of an afterlife, with the intention of the deceased mother to heal her daughter. With Heather now sobbing, I was doing all I could to be supportive while writing and trying to listen.

The boundaries of my rational mind were being shattered! Maybe, I found myself thinking, someone could come up with a few coincidental pieces of information about our relationship, but this medium did not know us in the slightest, and she had been precise about our two sons, our wedding, and my wife's mother. Plus, she had not known that Heather had come to the reading to connect with her mother. There were just too many facts for this to have been staged! Even being a skeptic at the time, I had seen firsthand evidence that the information was credible.

When it was my turn the reading was just as rewarding, with very specific information regarding my business and my grandfather, who had passed away some years earlier, as well as a helpful message for me about my marriage. Again, the medium began confidently saying, "I have a man standing here—he is older and saying he is your grandfather. Can you understand this?" I replied, "Of course"—none of my grandparents were alive anymore. She then described his death as "lonely and suffocating." This also made sense to me, as my grandfather had been in a nursing home by himself and had died from pneumonia. Next, the medium actually described the machines my grandfather had used to make dresses as a validation, proving this was whom she was speaking to. I realized that the only people in the world who were alive and knew this information were my parents, my brother, and myself. And none of us had ever met this woman before or even had talked with her.

Then the medium looked right through me and said, "Your grandfather says you're going to be okay—you've got nothing to worry about." Now *I* had tears in my eyes, as my recovery from cancer was still fresh in my memory. Here again, she shared very helpful information with me regarding my emotional state and was spot on. The messages for my wife and me were deeply personal and included things unique to each of us for our consideration.

When it was over and we were leaving her gallery, I thanked the medium, and that is when she turned back to me and said, "We have beginner's classes so you can learn more about this." This surprised me! Perhaps she knew something about me I was not yet aware of or, maybe she had picked up on my curiosity about all of it. I went home thinking about this experience and discovered that the temptation to learn more was irresistible. I had hoped that life is eternal, and now I fully believed it. Also, the experience had provided an emotional release for Heather, and some healing followed in the ensuing weeks. Eventually, I called the medium up and began the journey to what I call "wonderland."

## *Being Opened-Minded*

The whole experience seeing the medium was mind-blowing and out of my comfort zone to be sure. Yet I realized that maybe I didn't know everything there is to know and that I needed to discover more.

Upon my recovery, I promised myself to spend more time with my family and cherish my relationships with my two very young boys. I regarded myself as "lucky" to be feeling better and having a second chance, so I did not want to blow it. I consciously decided to peel back the layers of life and seek answers to deeper questions, and found that having a strong analytic mind and a natural inclination for research were useful tools to have in the process. By joining what the medium referred to as a "Circle," I would have a chance to satisfy my curiosity and to stretch my mind beyond the concepts it had previously held before.

One simple lesson in life I was learning was not to lose curiosity, as we never know the information and surprising knowledge we may encounter in a new experience. ❧ *The open mind is a humble mind and one that leaves room for expansion of new ideas. This in turn leaves room for creativity and wonder, which is the engine for evolution.* ❧

Now that my mind was open to new possibilities, the universe was responding and showing me things I had never expected existed. I was coming to see that, as the renowned physicist Albert Einstein once said, "the important thing is not to stop questioning. Curiosity has its own reason for existing."[3]

My curiosity and desire to know more regarding my health scare—understanding what may have caused it and where it almost took me—inflamed my passion for questioning. The rest was falling into place as if I was destined to follow this path.

CHAPTER 3

# THE CIRCLE: A BRIDGE TO ENLIGHTENMENT

*Every human being's purpose is identical: it's to "be" the spirit of God manifesting in the human condition. . . . Some teachers have referred to this shift in perception as going from seeing yourself as a human being, . . . struggling to have a spiritual experience, to knowing you are a spiritual being, having a divinely human experience. That's why we are here—to become that conscious vessel through which heaven touches earth!*

—Dennis Merritt Jones, *The Art of Being*

It's one thing to have a *belief* in God or a higher power, and it's another to have the actuality of it brought right to your doorstep. My experience with the medium had added a deeper sense of purpose to my life and revealed some possibilities as to why humanity is here. It opened the door to my becoming more aware of what reality may be. This led to more of my own questions and the idea that we live beyond our physical bodies.

I believe this is spirituality. It starts with a belief in an eternal life that is continuous. As was stated in my physics class in school, energy can neither be created nor destroyed. It continues. We never cease to exist even when we leave our physical bodies. So if we are spiritual, we believe that there is more than just the life we are now leading and that there will be still more after we die.

*It is important to emphasize that becoming spiritual does not mean that we have to give up believing in whatever religion we currently embrace. Truth may be found in many places as long as we also respect what is inside of us and respect other people's choices.* I found myself open to exploring this new avenue for seeking truth about the nature of existence.

## Back to School

Without much hesitation, I joined the teaching medium, Patricia Woods, and attended her weekly "Circle." Though Heather and I had encountered her together, I was the only one from my family attending. This was *my* journey.

As a new face to the Circle, I did not know what to expect. I felt excitement and trepidation all wrapped up into one. On the one hand, I embraced my curiosity and the need for exploration, but on the other hand, being there was out of my comfort zone.

The people who attended this weekly Circle group were from many career paths; they ranged from nurses, teachers, engineers, and social workers to psychologists, administrators, and financial specialists. All participants shared a common curiosity and a desire for learning. They were bright, well-educated people, and most had a natural skepticism and resistance to the work we pursued. We all had a common desire for exploring and to better understand ourselves and the Universal Intelligence that surrounds us.

The intent was for like-minded individuals to come together to learn and support each other as the Circle raised its energy vibration (frequency and power) each passing week with the

## The Circle: A Bridge to Enlightenment

development of its participants. *Consistency* each week is one key to raising the group's energy and building trust with each other as well as with the beings inhabiting the "other side," or the spiritual or nonphysical dimension.

One might assume that we needed to believe in life after death in order to take this class. Not true. As a beginner, this was not necessary; we just needed an open mind to see what might develop for us and our classmates.

We all had varying religious backgrounds and belief systems surrounding God, which was perfectly fine; none of this was ever questioned. I have come to understand that religion can actually be quite valuable for some, as it can lead to prayer and a closer relationship with one's Maker. However, even if in this case we were not religious and rather questioned a belief in God, as long as we were open and had a desire to learn, we could begin moving forward. This resulted in our becoming more sensitive and respectful to others around us.

The progress of each person in the Circle from week to week was unique. The results were highly personal, yet the group's energy vibration tended to rise over time with the development of each student. This is important, as our energy signature is that of low vibration being in physical form, while spiritual energy is of a higher vibration. As we completed the class exercises from week to week, we were able to begin sensing another reality that is with us all the time, yet hardly noticed.

There were approximately ten students in my particular Circle. The requirement of consistent attendance helped build the group's energy and provided discipline with the work we were going to learn. Each class usually had a meditation so we could relax ourselves to be more in harmony with the world around us. Several of the exercises and meditations that we did each week enabled us to shed some of the heavy emotional thoughts that weighed us down in our everyday lives.

We did exercises designed to stretch our psychic abilities, such as connecting to another person's energy field in the Circle and accessing personal information about him or her. The goal was to be as detailed as possible, even describing possible events from the past to really stretch our own intuition. Once we had participated in the Circle for six months to a year and were becoming more comfortable with the process of energy, we would take on more difficult exercises working with mediumistic exercises and the spiritual energy around us.

The meditations we experienced helped us go deep within ourselves to search for possible answers to our emotional blocks. On more than one occasion, as the meditation ended my eyes had tears, the result of confronting my fears and insecurities. Each week built upon some of the prior week's work. The more we attended the sessions, the more our own bodies and minds became clear, and the more we were attuned to the energy in the group.

The Circle is a reflection of its participants and the teacher who is leading it. The energy from each person is linked together with that of all the others, forming a higher energy signature than can otherwise be attained by sitting alone; this is then used for helping each other to do the exercises. The focus may be on psychic development, mediumship (contact with those who have passed), healing, trance, or some other modality in what is termed *metaphysics*, the study of the non-physical dimensions *beyond* the physical world in which we dwell. And within each of these modalities there are subsets or particular skill sets that correspond to each of these areas.

Each week when we all first arrived at the Circle, there could be some discussion of our experiences during the prior week and whether we had noticed anything different in our daily lives. Some of us were becoming more aware of our thoughts and more sensitive to the people around us. The meditations in particular grounded my racing thoughts and emotions, clearing the way for more awareness.

We would begin by closing our eyes and focusing on our breathing. A deep inhale was followed by a longer exhale, as we were exhaling the troubles of the day from our bodies. The focused breathing quieted our bodies and prepared us for a guided imagery designed to use our imagination in concert with our inner mind. This practice enabled each of us to expand our mind's boundaries, raise our energy, and clear emotional blocks.

Emotional memories can turn into stumbling blocks or become baggage when at any time in our life we experience a difficult situation that is not resolved in harmony. This is true for all of us. It does not matter what race or culture we are; we are all essentially emotional beings.

Examples of emotional blocks can be in the form of negative behavior patterns, such as anger, resentment, lack of trust, lack of confidence, fear, control, pain, hate, intolerance, impatience, and a number of others. It was interesting to me that none of us participating in this Circle had had any preconceived notions about changing anything about ourselves; the shifts just happened very naturally and at our own pace.

We learned in Circle that our bodies are comprised of energy centers, or "chakras," as they are called in Eastern traditions, which need to be open and working for us to properly develop our psychic abilities. Over time and with practice, these energy centers opened more for each of us. Ultimately, we were able to reach higher states of being, accessing our own energy within to develop psychically and even, for some, to develop "mediumship" skills to connect with the spiritual energy around us.

Meditations used in the Circles might take us back to a happier time in our lives or to a specific event where we had experienced a disappointment as a child. This process can help remove psychological obstacles we may have placed in our minds to protect ourselves at that time. Often, these mental or emotional protection mechanisms remain in the mind; through this type of exercise they can be shifted, making our own energy flow more effectively, and then we are more open to utilizing our intuition and other senses. The process is subtle and takes time, yet as our energy expands, it is precisely what is needed to open our psychic senses to be able to feel, hear, touch, see, and even smell what our ordinary senses may not perceive.

A key point to mention is that while these meditations were the same for everyone, the listening process was uniquely different for each individual. Every meditation allowed each of us to apply our own imagination to what we were hearing so that we could experience whatever was needed to rid ourselves of layers of emotional baggage. Every one of us has accumulated such memories to varying degrees, which is part of being human. It starts in childhood and builds throughout life. Removing these emotional layers and cluttered thoughts frees up the energy trapped within our physical being so that our real essence—our soul—may become more accessible to our everyday selves. Our soul has a purpose but our ego's role is finite, and often the bridge that connects these two is riddled with emotional debris, preventing a fluid exchange.

During one Circle we had a meditation that took us deep into a forest where there was a park bench near a stream. Imagining the sound of the stream was relaxing, while going deep into the woods was a metaphor for going down deep into meditation. Then we imagined an animal coming to speak with us at this bench. For me, a large brown bear came and offered me strength and wisdom. At first this image seemed trite, but then I realized what a difficult time I was going through in many areas of my life. In addition to some marital challenges, the economic collapse of 2008 was impacting me. Suddenly and inexplicably when I was emerging from this meditation, tears began streaming down my face. Out of all the possible animals I could have imagined, it was the strength of a bear for emotional and physical support that I most needed.

Following meditation and the opening of our energy centers, we usually went on to an exercise that was designed to stretch our psychic abilities by having us connect with and read, or interpret, someone else's energy in the Circle. This might consist of sensing something that might have occurred from someone's past, what is currently happening in this person's life, and a message for the future. All this can be picked up from someone else's energy, which is a fingerprint for that person from birth until death, storing all experiences. Prior experience was not a necessity; we each worked within our own capacity and ability.

In time and with enough development, most people can learn to use their psychic gifts of feeling, seeing, hearing, and knowing to read a person's energy field and perhaps even communicate with the normally unseen forces of the divine realm. It works as long as the *intent* is based on love and helping another human being and not on greed, selfish gain, or other dubious motivation. I learned that we *all* have these innate psychic abilities but are rarely ever taught how to use these inherent gifts.

## Stepping Stones

Before I began attending the Circle, I had been strong in my constitution and carried a fairly high level of adrenaline. As a business owner and head of a household, I did not think of this as out of the ordinary. In fact, it was typical of many

American entrepreneurs and, I suspect, other businesspeople residing elsewhere in the world.

After a year attending this spiritual Circle, my initial curiosity turned into commitment. I was very surprised that I actually found myself developing psychically, evolving my metaphysical senses while being more grounded emotionally than ever before. Although I was still uncertain about where this was going, I was aware that there were positive effects rubbing off on me from my involvement in this work. I just could not deny it.

There were changes taking place within me that were difficult to explain; all my perceptions were changing and the benefits were tangible. It was as if my own life was slowing down and I was standing still and sometimes *watching* chaos around me as I observed people. This was far different from my usual pattern of *participating* and *reacting* to the turmoil around me in my job as well as in my interactions on the streets of New York.

Another plus was that I was able to sleep better, and it also became difficult for me to stay angry with someone, which was also different from my usual past behavior. Even my patience improved during competition for a seat in my daily commute; New York can be a rough place at times, and with crowding at the commuter hubs, people naturally compete for space as they get on trains and buses.

While other people's difficult attitudes and emotional states of being used to tug at me, they were no longer registering with me. Previously, I would arrive home after a terribly busy day with little tolerance left. Now, however, if my wife had a problem on the home front, the news would roll right off of me, as I was realizing how little real impact trivial day-to-day upsets had on our life paths. I used to fight and bicker with her over small insignificant details, from dinner choices to where we may be going out at night. Now, I was being more empathetic and avoiding conflict, giving her the right of way, so to speak, and soon a wave of peace reigned over our home. Some might say we know this lesson: happy wife, happy life.

Even resentments that I had carried around like a badge of courage began to fall by the wayside. I became more comfortable in my own skin, not sweating the small stuff. Although I had formerly enjoyed dwelling on personal nonsense, it no longer served a purpose for me.

As I mentioned already, many Circle meetings took place during the fourth quarter of 2008, when the US economy and stock market were unraveling. Of course, I was strung out and could hardly eat after watching a six-hundred-point decline in the Dow Jones Industrial Average repeat itself, tick by tick, for several days in a row. Yet this spiritual work I was doing enabled me to stay focused and maintain balance in a gathering economic storm. The changes were also noticeable in others in the group who had life challenges far more gripping than my own.

People around me began acknowledging these shifts in myself as well. Family members and close friends first and then others found me calmer and more objective in my thoughts than they had previously remembered. This helped carry me through the financial crisis of 2008 and 2009 and allowed me to shoulder the fears of many of the people who came to me for financial advice.

Regarding the Circle, one may think that like-minded individuals can form a group and talk things out such as they do in therapy; even in Alcoholics Anonymous, people will feel better about themselves after sharing. However, this is not what was taking place during our time together in the Circle. There were deep changes occurring among all of us as we were learning to focus our minds and open our energies for a purpose. Ultimately, we learned that intelligence in the form of energy is always present and that we can direct a creative power within each of us to connect with this intelligence.

This experience, however, is unique for each individual and often depends on the *intent* and *focus* of the participants in the group. Everything is optional with regard to how much or how little we choose to embrace in any meditation. It depends on how our mind uses its imagination and is inspired by an unseen intelligence that resides in the energy surrounding us as well as in our individual soul.

The pace of this development is also different for people depending on their life experience and why they have come to do the work. In addition, this growth is sped up or slowed down by the individual's commitment and desire to learn and expand him- or herself.

☙ *Spiritual forces we cannot fully understand from our perspective also come into play. It is the spiritual energy working within the group from another realm, or dimension, that determines how much energy each person receives to help clear emotional layers. The stronger the emanation of these forces, the lighter we can become in our energy vibration.* ☙

Resolving an emotional block or releasing a memory through guided meditation does not always mean behavior modification, although it can happen for some people. It is about identifying and releasing emotional memories we all carry around. Negative emotions block our chakras, interfere with our thoughts, and sometimes cause us to get in our own way. Losing some of this baggage lightens and frees us, allowing us to be closer to our true selves. It helps us to be more objective in situations where previously we could not be.

As our objectivity with people, ideas, and opportunities increases, with less ego and confrontation, we can become open to things we may have missed before. This is powerful for

## The Circle: A Bridge to Enlightenment

living life fully. Certainly, we will have fewer stumbling blocks and be more authentic with our own intentions.

Interestingly, my motivation all along was to heal myself physically and reduce the chance of repeating my experience with cancer. All that I was learning in the Circle and its resultant multilevel benefits were most unexpected. Unintentionally, I discovered emotional healing for myself and an area of existence that provided answers to many of life's riddles!

The more I attended the Circle, the more grounded my emotions became. I was slower to become angry, if at all. But the effect was much more powerful than this. My emotional responses were tempered just enough that I actually became more disarming to others—taking the sword out of their hands rather than being typically aggressive. How transformational it could be if all of us could step back and see each other as equals and be more open to perceive the pain or suffering another person carries.

Emotionally, I had always been a little anxious and sensitive to those around me. Perhaps being high strung stemmed from my family life of strict upbringing during childhood and its effect on my thinking process. However, my sensitivity seemed more innate to the emerging person I was becoming and part of my deeper true self. I had thought that this part of me required protection, so I had purposefully tried to keep it hidden from the outside world. Sometimes, others had felt I was being closed, arrogant, or serious-minded when I was just trying to stay grounded and out of harm's way.

There are many parts of me that, as for others, have been formed by personal experiences throughout my life. These experiences, depending on their severity and the importance *I gave them,* shaped and molded who I am today. I have since learned that we can choose how we react to something by what meaning we give it and whether we believe it is worthy of an emotional response. By extension, if we believe we are hurt or have suffered, this will determine to what extent will we choose or avoid a future similar circumstance.

The accumulation of these experiences, our reactions, and future responses shapes our personality. ᛋ *We believe our personality is, in fact, who we are. We go to great lengths in life to preserve the integrity of this definition while seeking approval from the world around us.* ᛋ This is why we often repeat situations that may result in something negative. We are putting effort into gaining validation for creating what is essentially a false reality.

We have to ask ourselves if our "personality" that we shape a particular way is really who we are or whether it is just a cover for what is actually deeper inside us. This was one of the riddles I examined while in the Circle. Our answers were derived from introspection and not from some external formula.

In addition to opening ourselves up energetically to be able to see, feel, and communicate with the spiritual reality that surrounds us, one of the main objectives of the Circle was to be in a better position to help others—to be in service. As we become lighter in vibration, our awareness heightens within ourselves, as does our sensitivity to the world around us. With consistency and intent, this process can open all of our many psychic senses as we experience the energies surrounding us. I discovered that this was an important key to my development and not to be taken lightly. I had survived a physical crisis; now I wanted to evolve and learn more about my true nature.

Even at this early stage of curiosity, I began to realize how important a role emotional healing was playing in the fabric of my life. Previously unaware of my own behavior and how reactive I automatically was, I had been in a perpetual achievement and survival mode. I was not what one would call "in touch with my feelings."

This first step toward emotional healing simply happened through the process of clearing and expanding my awareness. There are plenty of good books published on this topic from authors such as Louise Hay, Wayne Dyer, and others. However, their words could not help me until I experienced it for myself and understood the real importance of healing emotionally.

We cannot just take an over-the-counter medicine or look into the mirror to fix our emotional state. It takes time. We may heal some of our physical symptoms, but if our emotional state is responsible for our physical state of being, then our original physical symptoms may return. The body is a wonderful barometer of buried feelings. ℘ *We may not have conscious awareness of what we are feeling, but the body always will.* ℘

The more emotional releasing that transpired from my participation in the Circle, the clearer was my perception of the world around me. What was truly surprising was that the awareness was not limited to my own life—I started to feel things about the lives of other people. It was something I couldn't even help or control. This applied to strangers and even those people I sometimes avoided for fear of confrontation. I began to see the interconnectedness of everyone and everything as if we were in one big dance together called life.

Our teacher often said, "Spirit wants a clean vessel." *Clean vessel for what?* I wondered. What do they want with me? The answer was the same thing God and our guides in heaven want for all people: *service*—for us to be helpful to our fellow humans. I have come to understand that service in one form or another is ultimately the highest form of work one can do during life.

Even if we do not identify ourselves as "spiritual," we may very well be in service to others. For example, have you ever stopped to wonder what led you to where you are in life? Or maybe why you feel as good as you do when helping another? It is the higher self, or "soul self," that provides the instincts you have within.

A benefit of clearing stuck emotional energy from our body is making room for something else to follow. This may include love for others or even developing more self-love. When we develop love for ourselves, we become better able to share with others the love we hold inside. ᛋ *It must start with us. Only then will this positive energy or love have the strength to be passed to those ready to receive.* ᛋ

The amazing thing about all this is I was the last person anyone would have expected to heal emotionally and physically through this process. Yet the truth is that I am like anyone else reading this book. We are all capable of embracing the deeper essence of who we truly are.

## *The Enlightenment*

The pages that follow provide greater details about the shift I experienced and the wonderful journey that we all are potentially able to experience. What's more, there are lessons we as citizens of this planet can learn and embrace that will lead each of us to a similar shift.

Many ideas in the remainder of this book came through me from my teachers and angels on "the other side"—heaven; I am only a vehicle for the expression of these words. There are those in the spiritual dimension who have been assisting us all along and desire to communicate important information to us at this time to help us move forward as a civilization. We are at a tipping point in history in many areas of our existence. It is these teachers and their love and compassion for the human race that foster the wisdom and practices that follow.

There may be a few people whose religious ideals begin running interference as soon as they hear the phrase "messages from beyond," preventing them from keeping an open mind. I was exactly the same way initially, yet over time I have been able to approach most all my experiences from a neutral point, allowing me to understand the information coming to and through me before reaching any conclusions. As one of many who has this ability I am only the messenger, and I am willing to share what these nonphysical guides teach.

Some people may say it is wrong to speak with those who have departed. Others, out of fear, will cite religious references as to why this cannot be so. If this is true for you, I ask you to please consider these souls to be angels, who would not waste time communicating information unless it was important to do so.

In the Bible there are references supporting communication with God as well as with what are called God's angels. Is there a difference between men five thousand years ago and the modern man of today? It was all right to speak to God or his helpers back then, but now it is questioned? Did God intend so many rules of what is right and what is wrong based on religious ideals? Did God intend people to define themselves by which religion they belong to? These things have sometimes served only to create differences among the peoples of the world when, truly, we are all the same in the Creator's eyes, having all emanated from the One Divine Source.

## Seven Principles for Clarifying Your Life Purpose

The next two parts of the book explore in detail seven simple steps for clarifying your life purpose. By following these principles, you will be embracing lessons for spiritual awakening that were given to me by guides in heaven. They are as follows:

1. Learn to love each other.
2. Understand that our thoughts and emotions are real energy that affects our health and that of others.
3. There is more power when we act as "one" people.
4. Learning is continuous, as the world is a school for the soul.
5. We incarnate from the Spirit realm to create.
6. God's helpers are always with us—no prayer is unheard.
7. You form your own reality.

I hope that you will be receptive to whatever is yours to learn. After all, you are not reading this book by "accident," but rather by divine purpose. There is clearly a reason you have been drawn to read this far already.

It is important to note that you are not your body, and you are not who someone has told you that you are. You are probably not even who you think you are. You are constantly evolving to be so much more than you have been previously; in fact, you are much more than you can even imagine. Self-actualization and coming to a state of oneness with the Creator is a long process. However, the journey is filled with love, fulfillment, and many uplifting treasures. There is no perfection expected here, only a willingness to be open to possibilities. You may be amazed at what you find out about yourself and your relationship to the vast universe beyond your senses. I invite you to join me.

PART TWO

# Can You Imagine?

*Knowledge of what is possible is the beginning of happiness.*
—George Santayana, brainyquote.com

CHAPTER 4

# PRINCIPLE ONE:
# LOVING EACH OTHER

> *A loving person lives in a loving world. A hostile person lives in a hostile world. Everyone you meet is your mirror.*
> —Ken Keyes Jr., quotationspage.com

I have had opportunities to communicate with those residing in the spiritual dimension, either on my own or through people who have done this work for many years. The two points they repeat over and over again are "Be at peace within your own minds" and "Practice universal love." In essence they are saying that in the brief amount of time we have here on Earth, we need to find peace within ourselves and love for each other.

Synchronistically, according to Raymond A. Moody, Jr., MD, the bestselling author of *Life After Life*, people who return from near-death experiences also tell us that in the seeming closing moments of their earthly lives they learned that the most important thing we can do while here is to learn to love.[1] Loving without asking for anything in return began taking place in me after looking deep within myself and discovering a gap that existed between who I thought I was and the reasons my soul incarnated.

## A Lighter Heart

One way to find inner peace and to have a more loving heart is to find the connection to our own light, or soul, which resides within us. As I continued attending the Circle and experiencing what the teacher called "development," which assists in this very process, I felt my own heart become unburdened from past experiences. I had had many scars from previous relationships that had soured and disappointments in business that I had held on to until my own heart had hardened. It was closed for many years when I was single because I thought that protecting myself in this way would keep me from getting hurt. Instead, this had the opposite effect: it kept me from experiencing a deeper love that we all deserve to experience.

As a result of the spiritual development I was doing, over time I began feeling lighter within and began to love more freely and unconditionally without asking for anything in return. This had not always been my experience—many times I had either secretly or overtly desired something from the other person or situation and was disappointed when my efforts were not reciprocated. It felt good to break from my past patterns that no longer were serving me.

Learning to love more unconditionally benefits both parties, I discovered. One might think that the receiver of the love energy would benefit the most, but really the reward is more for the person giving the love—he or she experiences a lighter, higher energy vibration in their own being. I did not realize this until I experienced it firsthand, with my own heart really opening up. In particular, I volunteered for three years in a hospice organization, where I kept patients company. Many of these people had very few visitors, and some were very close to death. It brought joy to me knowing that they had someone near them at a frightening time when they faced what they perceived as "the end" of their existence.

This was a different kind of love from what I had experienced in my more intimate relationships, in which the old axiom "Love is blind" tended to show up at some point. I found that when we remove sexual thoughts that can cloud our judgment, as well as selfish thoughts and desires, what remains is simply pure "love" for anyone or anything. And an incredible thing begins to happen: there is little room for judgment or the thought, *What's in it for me?*

Amazingly, a space within this interaction is created for anything to happen, as our usual guarded selves are given the freedom to *be*. Creativity is fostered, and the people giving of themselves usually end up receiving unexpected gifts in the process. *As we give our love and energy to another, we actually place ourselves in a position of receiving love and energy back.*

This concept may seem simple to apply in a close relationship, but it also applies in reference to our fellow humans. Try this with an acquaintance, a stranger on the street, a coworker, a rival, or even an animal. Do not worry if this energy is not returned to you instantly—you have created space for it to do so, and, amazingly, eventually it will. This process works!

Try being aware of when your ego is attempting to insert itself and instead try to be selfless in your thoughts with others. If you can be more generous, compassionate, caring, helpful, patient, and sympathetic—not from being submissive or weak but from an authentic place of support—these qualities will likely be expressed back at you. And even if your actions do not appear to be reciprocated, you are doing the important work of carrying yourself from day to day with an *open heart* toward other human beings, and this benefits the entire planet. As author and teacher Dr. David McKinley says, "It's not your position in life; it's the disposition you have which will change your position."[2]

Contrary to popular belief, deep down there is little difference between you and other people, as we all originate from the same Divine Source. It is our learned behaviors that have led us to false perceptions of the truth, which then leads to an experience of separation. Just as we all came into this world naked, we will be this way again when we arrive at the "other side" without our possessions. We may travel different paths in this lifetime while healing ourselves, but eventually we arrive at the same destination. In Hebrew, there is a prayer called the Shema, which says, "Hear O Israel, the Lord our God, the Lord is One."[3] Regardless of our religious beliefs, this prayer is saying there is only one God, and as God is present in every one of us, we are all one people.

How is God present in all of us? It is widely believed scientifically, and by some religions, that the universe started long ago from the same energy source and it just keeps expanding; this is what is known as the big bang theory.[4] I know of spiritual healers who study the Kabbalah, the mystical teachings of Judaism, and repeat the Shema prayer in an effort to raise the energy in a room before beginning to heal others.

## *Walking Your Own Line*

As a species, we seem to compartmentalize our love for other people, places, and things; we are careful about sharing ourselves with others. It is more than just being caught up in our day-to-day activities; there is a lack of trust with one another and too many fears within us that we might be hurt. We are so protective of our hearts that often there is little room for genuine friendship to be exchanged between strangers and even with those who are most dear to us.

Some of us may not have grown up in loving families, or we were told negative things that were not true about ourselves, but we believed them anyway and then felt we were undeserving. Feelings of unworthiness and low self-esteem may also creep in when we look at the world around us and start thinking that others have more than we do. This lack of love for ourselves can escalate over time, and we may find that being hard on ourselves becomes one of our main modes of operation. Feelings of unworthiness or low self-esteem lead to an illusion that we must always protect ourselves from others. Anger, fears, anxieties, and heartaches may lead us to creating a false reality, which can have us yield to disempowering ways of being, such as depression, alcoholism, and drug-taking.

We must ask ourselves, do these reactions really accomplish anything? If we become angry, for example, this feeling and its side effects impact us worse than the one at whom we are angry—they create disharmony in our body, mind, heart, and spirit.

Fear can be all encompassing when it takes hold. When one is in fear, most other emotions are dominated by it. Certainly, love is difficult to experience if one is coming from fear. Compassion, another key to opening the heart, is not present with fear. Fear is a false identity that takes over when we believe we are less than we are. ❧*And since we tend to attract what is most like us, rather than what is different, if we live in fear, we will likely attract more fear, which continues to propel the cycle. Likewise, if we surround ourselves with love, this is what we will attract. Like begets like; this is the law.* ❧

Look around you. Take notice of people or groups that band together, as well as places where particular types of people congregate, and you will begin to notice how true this is. People tend to like to be with others they think are like them—it makes them comfortable to feel they belong.

If you look at your own life and observe the people with whom you surround yourself, you can see this lesson in action. How do you feel about the working of this law in your life? Are you happy with your choices? Do they serve your highest interests?

You choose your own reality. If you are at peace with the life you are living and operating with an open heart, this is a positive place to be; in this case, you may ask what else you can do to further your empowering life experiences. However, if you are not at peace, then you are responsible for making any changes needed for moving you forward. You can decide right now how you want to live, and those will be the signals you send out to others. In time, new people will enter your life who reflect the energy and choices you are living.

## Keys to Open the Heart

Through my Circle work I have learned that there are secrets to opening and expanding our heart center, which is a storehouse of energy for our soul. The following two words, *acceptance* and *tolerance*, if mastered properly, will assist you on your life path and enable you to progress more fully.

### Acceptance

Mastering acceptance is a potential road to finding inner peace. If we hold on to heartache and disappointment long enough, this inhibits us from loving and accepting ourselves and, by extension, others. Having experienced this many times, I have learned that it is best to acknowledge the pain we have experienced, learn from mistakes, and move on. Other than fueling our own ego, there is no point in being stubborn and holding onto negativity when we can flow with life's energy rather than resisting it.

Acceptance needs to start within us and then move outward. I know people who are enormously successful in the business world yet are not accepting of themselves. Ironically, it is the lack of acceptance and inner discomfort within themselves that pushes them minute by minute, day by day. Each morning they wake up and off they go, working to prove to themselves and everyone else that they are worthy. This propels them to go beyond what other people normally consider average performance. Over time, however, they learn that money cannot buy happiness, and many of these same people lack inner peace. What's more, they often have compromising relationships with others.

People are caught up each day focusing on imperfections in themselves (and others). Yet the truth is that we are *all* imperfect . . . period. For that matter, my understanding from spirit communication is that the universe is imperfect, meaning that there will always be ways we can grow and evolve to better express our divine purpose. So why spend so much energy focusing on imperfections when we could be putting that energy into making a positive contribution to the world?

Do not ever put yourself down when comparing yourself with others. Lessons take many forms, as we all are at different stages of development. We are all unique, so our challenges and predicaments will always be different. This is why we should never judge another person. We cannot begin to understand what it is to be another person and walk in his or her shoes. We cannot understand from our human perspective where another is in life. Whether you are rich or poor, you may find lessons of compassion and faith along your path.

Appearances on the outside can mask problems people have underneath it all; we often see examples of this in the news. We may have found ourselves a bit envious or jealous at first, only to ultimately be thankful for what we already have. We are each on a unique path, and we should live it as fully as possible, rather than trying to imitate others or believe that their life is more meaningful than ours.

We also need to be careful about feeling superior to others. Too often, we believe that our views are more important than someone else's, and so we feel there is little reason to be accepting of that person; this is our ego getting in the way of possibilities. We can see this operating every day in various situations, from those involving the common man on the street to large corporations and even big governments. Too many of us think that what we believe in is the truth, and we allow little room for a differing point of view. Before we know it, we are in a fight with others over trivial matters.

Too many never come to terms with who or where they are in life and do not feel empowered to identify what might need to be changed. Instead, they find it easier to blame others for their predicaments. This can be a vicious cycle that is hard to break. We particularly see this when it comes to relationships. Men and women often blame each other when things do not go right, and, sadly, even children blame their parents for their own misfortunes when things do not work out for them later in life. However, we must each take responsibility for who and what we are.

To be more accepting of another creates harmony; more importantly, it avoids disharmony within oneself. "If I could define enlightenment briefly, I would say it is the quiet acceptance of what is,"[5] says motivational speaker and author Dr. Wayne Dyer.

However, no one is suggesting that you become accepting to the point of being submissive. You do not have to accept your situation, whatever it may be; it is always good to make improvements by pushing yourself further. Learn to be honest with yourself about who you are and whatever your situation is. This acceptance is a critical piece to begin the process of empowering change and becoming more tolerant of other people. It is better to build bridges with those around you rather than tearing them down.

*Principle One: Loving Each Other*

*Tolerance*

As acceptance helps one navigate his or her heart internally, tolerance helps to navigate one's heart outward within the world. As we become more tolerant of one another, we create a space for creativity and eventually freedom for change. In addition, the qualities of acceptance and tolerance assist us in becoming more patient, which also enhances our relationships with others.

More tolerance in the world can lead to great strides in evolution, instead of the warlike behavior we too often see around us. You may not like everyone you meet, but you need to respect and honor other people's rights. Counsels seventeenth-century writer and philosopher Voltaire, "We are full of weakness and errors; let us mutually pardon each other our follies."[6] Compassion for others may follow once you begin to soften your heart and become tolerant of your neighbor.

The lessons of compassion and forgiveness can more easily be assimilated and implemented once acceptance for oneself and tolerance for others have been embraced. It can be difficult having compassion for another if you have none for yourself.

We are intolerant of others because at times we fear what we don't know and because of our own egos. We assume we are right in one area of our lives because we know we are smart in other areas. Our personality may be well meaning, so this behavior is unintentional, but it still persists, and as the ego continues to grow it causes us to get in our own way. According to author Anais Nin, "We don't see things the way they are. We see things the way *we* are."[7]

It is difficult to stay objective with others if we are emotionally based in our thinking. However, our ability to give others the benefit of the doubt and to stay neutral will create the possibility for more meaningful interactions.

We are not meant to be an island to ourselves. A lack of tolerance for others often becomes the seed for closing off and separating ourselves from the world around us. "Indeed," says professor, psychologist, and author Dr. Carl Jung, "a person can be so identified with his ego that he loses the common bond of humanity and cuts himself off from others. As nobody wants to be entirely like everybody else, this is quite a common occurrence."[8] This is the exact opposite of our natural state as spiritual beings, which is one of connection to "all" on the other side of the veil. Connections with others are paramount for a meaningful existence.

Intolerance for others creates separation that eventually will need correction, and life lessons to bring this about can be hard to bear. It is always easier making changes now rather than waiting until things are so stuck that there is just too much pain involved to break out of them.

## The Time Is Now

Time is running out for solving our differences with each other and with our neighbors across the globe. The global population continues to expand, and basic resources such as energy and food are in demand like never before. Geological catastrophes, once rare, are becoming more commonplace, forcing us to rely even more on one another. Nuclear energy and the ability to create nuclear weapons are potentially getting into the hands of those who value the religious beliefs of their cultures more than their own lives, and so the lives of others are less important than adhering to their ideals.

There are too many people around the world demonstrating violence toward others. Rather than denounce anyone in particular, one only needs to look at the world news each day to recognize this way of being. This survivalist mentality is a destructive force, cutting us off from each other rather than all of us working together to find creative solutions to world problems. We must let go of this if we are to evolve and move forward.

When working with those in spiritual form, I have learned that "love" is the common language that crosses all barriers. It is a powerful force used by them to bring about healing and change with those who will accept it. It is our responsibility to bring love, acceptance, and tolerance into our relationships and interactions with others; these are all vital to establishing peace on our planet and its ultimate survival. Everything is interconnected, and the time to act is now.

CHAPTER 5

## PRINCIPLE TWO:

# Thoughts and Emotions Are "Alive"

*You think you're one of a special breed; you think that you're his pet Pekinese. I'll be your savior, steadfast and true; I'll come to your emotional rescue.*

—Mick Jagger/Keith Richards, "Emotional Rescue"

In the mid-twentieth century, Russian scientists Semyon Kirlian and his wife, Valentina, were doing research in photography. They developed a technique called Kirlian photography, which permitted the camera lens to capture images of energy fields from living matter.[1] This proved *scientifically* that all creatures have a vibrant energy surrounding them, separate from the physical. This energy field is referred to as the "aura."[2]

When it comes to the human energy field, it contains all of our thoughts and emotions. As we are thinking and feeling, this is always being reflected in our aura. Although this energy is not living tissue, it has a life of its own. During my training in Circle, I could at times see a person's aura, feel and even psychically read their aura, and know personal information just from connecting with their energy field. Connecting to someone else's energy field is done with *intention*, using your own heart energy or energy directed from your mind. With practice, you may be able to connect to other parts of the auric field to access information the body stores at various physical locations. Many of the psychic exercises in class were specifically designed for us to master the art of connecting to and reading another person's energy field.

Think for a moment how you feel when entering a room during a heated argument. How does the energy feel? Perhaps it feels heavy and a bit uncomfortable, so you want to leave the room just as quickly as you are able. By contrast, what happens when you enter a room where people are laughing and loving each other? It feels welcoming and light, and often a smile takes hold on your own face. The emotional energy in a room gets picked up by anyone who wanders in and can also affect you. Incredibly, other people's energy can attach to your energy, pass right through you, and even take on a life of its own, seeming almost tangible, before dissipating.

Human beings are by definition "emotional." Exploring these emotions, which we all have, is part of our human experience. However, while emotions serve the purpose of expression, another important aspect is the *releasing* of this energy. If one's emotions are withheld and turned inward, potentially more harm than good may ensue. When emotional memories earlier in life become buried deep in our tissues without our conscious awareness, it can have an affect on our behavior. Even worse, it can cause harm to our physical bodies. This stuck energy gets in the way of our own normal energy flow and can even block energy centers, or "chakras," in the body. (More detailed information about the chakras follows later in this chapter.) If this happens for an extended period of time, disease may follow. *This is the significance of knowing that emotions are energy that needs releasing.*

*Principle Two: Thoughts and Emotions Are "Alive"*

Having a lack of self-worth in childhood and being shy earlier in life, I repressed my emotions, being fearful of being rejected for expressing myself. This may have led to stomach issues, as this is where the third chakra, which stores these emotional issues, is located. Later in life, my storing of fear and stress in the adrenals likely contributed to my kidney cancer in the second-chakra area of my body.

## *Releasing the Past*

From my years of working on Wall Street and seeing a revolving door of so many people coming and going and opportunities passing me by, I carried anger and resentment around as if it were a badge of courage to wear on my chest. What purpose did this serve? Nothing, except some sort of false expectation I had of the world around me possibly taking notice. Did anyone else care? No. And eventually neither did I anymore—it was wasted energy and I was focused on what I perceived as the bigger picture of where life was taking me. My attention turned to the more spiritual dimensions for fulfillment.

As curiosity turned into habit, my flirtation with spirituality and seeking answers for my own healing became a weekly commitment. No longer was I just intellectualizing spirituality, I was beginning to live it. There was no denying how well I felt physically, as well as the powerful changes that were taking place inside of me emotionally. Although I could still be pulled in many directions, especially at my day job, the stresses and strains that normally had taken their toll on me from work could no longer grow roots. I was becoming more grounded in my emotions and more focused in my thoughts about others and their well-being. Even some of the old heartaches from my youth dissipated, and a lightness of being was taking hold.

Regardless of what the issues are for you, your emotions—if they are strong enough and not given a proper resolution—can leave residue in your body. Science has already discovered links between anger and heart disease.[3] We all experience some frustration and negative emotions from time to time; this is normal. However, when our emotions are intense they need to be released. If not resolved, they can become buried within us for years, creating energy blocks, discomfort, and even illness. For example, when I went through periods of fear and stress, my immune system shut down and I found myself on antibiotics many times. *If we do not come to terms and accept the circumstances of an emotional situation and properly communicate and express our feelings, the issues literally get stuck in our tissues.*

In 1976 motivational author Louise Hay published a book that brought attention to the relationship between our emotional and mental patterns, and how this can potentially cause illness. The current edition is called *Heal Your Body*, and it is an interesting guide to ailments with their corresponding underlying mental patterns. The book indicates that a change in one's thoughts and behaviors can result in a change to one's underlying health and the lessening of a particular illness. While recovering from cancer, I used this book as a reference and even more so while I was in development attending Circle. This material was a useful guide as I focused on my illness and pains and the corresponding releasing of emotions I believed were being held within my body.

Hay says, "When I hear about someone's illness, no matter how dire their predicament seems to be, I know that if they're willing to do the mental work of releasing and forgiving, almost anything can be healed."[4] And, this is exactly how I conducted myself—by forgiving everyone I could, from my parents for being overbearing while I was growing up to even

*Principle Two: Thoughts and Emotions Are "Alive"*

ex-girlfriends or old bosses when in the end things might not have ended well. Each time I forgave someone, my heart felt lighter and lighter. So forgiving led to healing emotionally, and ultimately I felt better physically.

The teacher and medicine man White Eagle, in the channeled book *Spiritual Unfoldment 1*, also expresses the power of our thoughts to impact us very specifically on many levels:

> Thought can create good health, and can heal; but it can also inflict pain and disease, and it can disrupt and destroy the bodily, mental and soul life. Science has only reached the outermost fringe in comprehending the power of thought. Thoughts of anger, fear and hate form the root of all suffering and of all wars. Thought can also bring forth beauty, harmony, brotherhood and all else humanity longs for.[5]

One of the themes in the Edgar Cayce readings is that the physical, mental, and spiritual aspects of oneself are actually all related. These bodies are not separate from each other, but rather they interact and affect each other in ways we are only now beginning to understand. In "Reading 2812-1," Cayce put it this way: "There is the physical body, the mental body, and the soul, or spiritual body. They each have their environs. They each have their attributes. But they are one."[6] In truth, everything is interconnected in the universe and within ourselves.

According to scholar, mystic, and author Dr. Ernest Holmes, "thoughts are things"—they are real and have a life of their own, from which all else follows.[7] It works this way: Your *mind* starts with a *thought*, then a *feeling* occurs within you from this thought, which is followed by your *emotions*, which are released with outward behavior or not discharged and then held within your physical body. If you can control your thoughts, then your feeling, emotional, and physical patterns will follow suit.

Here is an example of how this process works: I have a friend who is a financial officer for an organization, and he informed board members that finances were not so good. In response to his perceived "alarmist" attitude, he was told that he could no longer give the financial report to the larger community at an annual meeting. Since in his mind he was just being honest, his *thought* was that the board was not appreciating his work. His *feeling* was that he was hurt by the lack of trust from other board members, and this triggered old self-esteem issues. His *emotions* that followed were anger, resentment, and even revenge! All of this manifested *physically* in him not sleeping well at night and his relationship with this group being full of conflict and disharmony.

But the story doesn't end there. My friend has done spiritual work for many years and understood that if he could *change his thinking* about this situation, there could be a different outcome. He came to realize that his thoughts were toxic, both for him and the organization, and he needed to do something about this. He was able to *shift his thinking* and see this whole experience as a "blessing in disguise," since in truth he had been unhappy and unfulfilled as the treasurer for a couple of years and had been thinking that it was time to move on and turn his attention to more creative ventures, and this situation provided the impetus to do so. With this revised perspective, he decided to give up his financial role. His *feeling* changed to one of relief, and his *emotion* moved to gratitude for the new possibilities that were open to him. This is manifesting *physically* for him as sleeping well again and even losing weight, more harmonious and peaceful interactions with fellow board members, and excitement about potential new endeavors, which are already flowing toward him.

The mind always starts with the thoughts first, and the chain reaction flows from there; the choice is up to us which way

*Principle Two: Thoughts and Emotions Are "Alive"*

we go. Positive and healthy thoughts create positive feelings, healthy emotions, and, ultimately, more balance and harmony in our outer experience. See in your own life how this is true. We are emotional creatures, so you must be patient with yourself. It took me five years of diligent work and I am still striving to be in control of my thoughts.

## *The Aura*

The aura is an energy field emanating from within us and directing outward in many directions and colors. According to author Cyndi Dale, the aura is our biomagnetic field, which conveys information taking place inside the body rather than on the skin.[8] It will go wherever you direct your intention. This is why if you are staring at people they often will turn and look in your direction or right at you—it is because you are directing your energy at them. They feel it but are usually not sure what it is they are feeling until they see you looking at them.

During my time in development I studied "hands-on healing" and the physical aspects of the dynamic energy field that surrounds each of us. I discovered what it was like to literally *feel* the energy field of another person. In time, I could pass my hands about an inch above someone lying down and understand where there were energy blocks in that person's aura. With practice, I could also understand what the underlying problem was that was causing the variation in energy around the person. Often it was an emotional issue that was being reflected in the energy field. Sometimes, it was an old broken bone that had left a small energy scar that could be felt as a tingling point in the energy field. This experience and others in my development work ultimately convinced me that I was onto something big that people needed to know more about.

Over time, I became a conduit for directing this energy for helping others; I was able to clear their aura field of stuck emotional energy. It is important to note that the energy being directed is always from a divine source that is based on love; this is not a magical power.

Just like with the Kirlian photography example mentioned earlier, we each have energy within us and layers of energy surrounding us. Each layer represents information about who we are. There are a number of teachers in healing fields and many who write books presenting this information. Two in particular offering good insights are Steven Thayer, who has a healing technique called "Integrated Energy Therapy,"[9] and Barbara Brennan, in her healing book *Hands of Light*.[10] Without getting too technical, both of these authors agree that there are several energy layers in the aura surrounding the human body, and each layer carries specific knowledge that contains the past, present, and future information about us. It even reflects disease in the physical body. As our thoughts and emotions change, so does the energy surrounding our physical being.

In the aura, there is an *emotional layer* that carries our feelings, emotions, and traumas. There is a *mental layer* that is influenced by our thoughts, beliefs, and attitudes. There is also a *spiritual layer* of energy, which is a reflection of our link with the Creator, our beliefs, and why we are here at this time on Earth. All three layers can affect our energy field and interact with our mind and physical body. And all three layers can be influenced as our mental patterns and emotional attitudes change.

People with a psychic sense for seeing energy, which is called "clairvoyance," have the ability to see this energy with all the glory of light and color. For example, if you are deep in thought, the color of your aura may be yellow; if you are in

## Principle Two: Thoughts and Emotions Are "Alive"

pain or are angry, it may turn red; and if you are in love, there may be shades of pink visible. A majority of the psychics I know say they see the colors of the aura this way. So your aura is living energy, as your emotions are indeed *alive* in these layers that surround you.[11]

Part of the process of clearing our emotional layers is restoring the body's free flow of energy to the auric energy field surrounding us. Scientists and others have discovered that as energy flows more freely, there are fewer blocks and distortions in the body and our energy and health can improve. Western medicine is now discovering this to be true, although Eastern medicine has known this for centuries! The healing modality of acupuncture reflects this knowledge, with its emphasis on removing energy blocks through a system of energy meridians found throughout the body.

The main energy centers, or chakras, are located in the human body along a line starting at the base of the spine and rising up to the top of the head. The first, or "root," chakra is at the base of the spine. The second chakra, also called the sacral chakra, is located about two inches below the belly button. The third, or "solar plexus," chakra is in the upper abdomen in the stomach area. The fourth, or "heart," chakra is in the center of the chest, just above the heart. The fifth, or "throat," chakra is at the throat. The sixth chakra, also called the "third eye" or "brow" chakra, is located in the middle of the forehead slightly above the eyebrows. At the very top of the head is the seventh, or "crown," chakra.

Our lower energy centers—the first, second, and third chakras—are receptors for receiving energy flow from the Earth. As this energy travels up through our legs and passes through the lower levels of the body, it can ignite our own energy. The energy continues upward through the heart, throat, brow, and top of the head. This life force is the essence of what we receive from the planet we live on, and it helps sustains us.

The heart chakra, the fourth, is a tremendous storehouse of energy for people; it is connected with our ability to love and such emotions as joy and inner peace. However, it is also one of the places where emotional issues can interfere with the body's normal activities.

The upper chakras—the fifth, sixth, and seventh—have many uses and are where people derive the ability for communication with the spiritual dimensions of existence and the Creator. These chakras will not work as well for spiritual work if the lower chakras are clogged with emotional issues. This is why most people need to clear out the emotional issues in these lower energy centers by eliminating the emotional debris in the first four chakras. As this energy is cleared our energy vibration becomes lighter, enabling us to sense and feel the finer energies that already surround us. (See Appendix A for additional details about the chakras.)

In some cases, these energy centers are blocked in people. Emotional issues, frustrations, anger, stress, life pressures, unhappiness, and disempowering thoughts lead to the closing down of our energy receptors. When these centers (chakra points) are closed by emotional debris, the natural energy flow is cut off within the body. This can result in low vitality, imbalances of energy, and even a predisposition for illness and disease in the areas where the energy blocks are.[12]

## *Innate Instincts*

Babies are born with a connection to the Divine. While verbal communication is not possible, their eyes and physical behaviors tell a different story. If you want to witness authentic behavior that is unfiltered by ego or societal pressures, watch

*Principle Two: Thoughts and Emotions Are "Alive"*

a baby. You will see joy and laughter, hugging, kissing, anger, pain, and crying without thought for itself and whether it is all right to feel a certain way. In time, as the baby assimilates with its environment, parents, siblings, and other connections, it begins to modify its behavior.

As babies grow and their interactions and life experiences increase, so does their emotional range expand, both in positive ways and negative, with disappointments, frustrations, and anger, and so on. Ego is formed. Emotionally, children's connection with their physical environment becomes the overriding force. Their natural connection with the Divine fades or recedes to a more inaccessible place deep within. And while this divinity, spark, or soul remains inside all of us, there is rarely a second thought of what role it plays or how we may access this power. We identify with what is tangible even though what is *intangible* is the greater power.

## Shielding the Heart

Before being married and before doing any spiritual work, my own heart was heavy for many years, as I've mentioned; I found it difficult to maintain close relationships. While single, I had several long-term relationships that had gone sour and even a broken wedding engagement, and unconsciously I began shutting my heart down for self-preservation and a fear of being hurt. Years later in Circle, some feelings attached to these old negative circumstances from my past began surfacing and releasing. Meditations led by the teacher often touched me deeply in ways that could not be felt when my ego was wide awake guarding my feelings. The result was the releasing of buried emotions, such as anger and frustration and the freeing of this blocked energy, which began to restore the well-being of my aura.

Many of us, particularly in Western societies, too often lead with our heads and not our hearts. For years, I was a master in primarily thinking with my head rather than feeling with my heart. Life moves at a fast pace from moment to moment, especially with advances in technology, and one has to make a conscious decision to slow the mind, as it is easy to get weighed down with all the information coming at us from e-mails, cell phones, and other technological devices. Our emotional responses sometimes get ignored with all this mental activity.

In 1925 an interesting conversation took place between Dr. Carl Jung and an enlightened Native American chief of the Taos Pueblo named Ochwiay Biano ("Mountain Lake"). Besides being a famous psychologist, Dr. Jung traveled constantly, observing people, places, and things, and his path had taken him to Taos, New Mexico.

Dr. Jung and Chief Ochwiay Biano were discussing the differences between Indian and white American cultures when the chief had this to say: "See how cruel the whites look. Their lips are thin, their noses sharp, their faces furrowed and distorted by folds. Their eyes have a staring expression; they are always seeking something; they are always uneasy and restless. We do not know what they want. We do not understand them. We think that they are mad. They think with their heads!" To which Dr. Jung replied, "Why of course. What do you think with?" And Chief Ochwiay Biano responded, "We think here," pointing to his heart![13] In some ways this is such a simple idea, yet this conversation reveals a profound observation of different ways of being.

The meditative work and spiritual exercises I did in Circle continued to release stuck energies that were still in my body. From time to time, I also made visits to alternative energy healers to work with my body's energy layers, helping to release even more of these blocks. In fact, there are energy healers throughout the world with mediumistic abilities that work with God's heavenly helpers. They possess the skill and talent for acting as a conduit between the divine energies and those in need of healing. The truth is that many of us are capable, if the intention and integrity are there, of learning how to be a conduit for these healing energies.

## Emotional Development

The journey of releasing and evolving is a process that for me required discipline and patience. My active work was over a five-year period, although the learning and growing never stops. Transformation is not something that happens overnight; it takes time, especially for someone like me, who was dug in and inflexible in my thoughts and beliefs for so long. I reserved one night a week for Circle for approximately 250 weeks, and this commitment was worth every moment.

From this expansion of my being more harmony entered into my life, and I became more even tempered. I became slower to move into anger, more compassionate with strangers, and far more patient with my boys, who are like lion cubs. I found myself giving food to people living on the street and giving more money to those less fortunate. There had always been a sensitive side to my personality, but now I was not afraid to show it and share it with others. Over time, as I began feeling lighter, more intuitive, and more centered, the whole process of development became gratifying and took on a deeper meaning.

Ironically, I was not becoming weak, as might have formerly been a concern, but rather I actually felt more emotionally steady and able to carry myself more confidently than ever before. Nor was I less sensitive; in fact, I was *more* sensitive, but to issues that really mattered to me. Heart issues had always been important, but the little things that had usually set me off no longer had as much hold on me. Taking buses and trains around New York, as often as I did, provided many opportunities for being in close proximity to people. In the past, I had almost wanted to pull the hair out of my head, if not someone else's, when I got bumped or someone was loud or stepped in front of me to take the one seat I had just been about to sit in. Now, I gently allowed others to be without feeling a need to respond from a perceived need to defend. Surprisingly, I began to appreciate the differences in others and saw them as the Creator expressing itself rather than feeling that if people were different from me, then something might be wrong with them (or me).

Many of us protect ourselves from people we do not know and are on guard to the differences between them and us. Once we assess this, we determine to what degree we can be ourselves around them and how protective we need to be with our hearts and our emotional selves. ✼ *However, imagine what it would be like if we all saw each other as being more similar rather than different—how much less effort and energy would be spent on protecting ourselves and how much more fulfilling our interactions would be with each other.* ✼

### False Imprisonment

A lot of people in this world are busy trying to compete and get ahead in one way or another. In the fast-paced environment where many of us reside, it is easy to allow feelings of fear and inadequacy to find their way into our thoughts. The technology and information revolution that is sweeping the globe puts news sensationalism in front of us at every turn.

As we live in a world that is dominated by money and looks, and a society that worships what people *have*, a natural

## Principle Two: Thoughts and Emotions Are "Alive"

competition is created. This competition then gives birth to the emotions of anger and resentment, where many ache with desire and want. On the other hand, those who have what others want and are what society deems "successful" may have dominating thought patterns, resulting in an existence based on themselves.

I speak from experience. Being successful financially before the age of thirty brought me an inflated ego. Several years later I was almost broke, scrambling to make ends meet, and was now looking at others who had passed me by. It was a dose of humble pie that luckily took place at a youthful age. Having experienced both sides of this coin, these are lessons I know well.

Although these emotional thought patterns and life experiences of inferiority and superiority appear to be on opposite ends, they both potentially create false mental imprisonments. On one end, many supposedly "have-nots" walk around feeling unworthy, while on the other end, the supposed "haves" think others are not good enough for them. The truth is that neither of these realities are accurate—they are self-imposed mental patterns of false imprisonment. ❧ *The experience of the human condition is based on a false pretense of a society that decides ahead of time what is valuable for its inhabitants. At a another time in history or in another culture, there would be a whole different set of false pretenses of what is important for the members of its society.* ❧

Ironically, most human beings try to conform to their culture's values for acceptance even though in heaven, when our physical shells drop away, none of these specific patterns exist, as we are all from the same divine source. So much energy is expended during our lifetimes trying to make others conform to our ways of being when, in fact, the diversity of humankind is a spiritual gift that should be embraced rather than judged—we are each a unique expression of Spirit in form.

## *Internalizing*

Many times I have asked why I suffered the kidney cancer and whether there was a link to my emotional side, where I internalized my frustrations from work and my personal life. My anger, resentment from career pressures, and even fear might have ultimately pushed others away and taken its toll on my body.

According to Rosalyn Bruyere, a respected and prominent energy healer, "most inflammatory diseases, no matter where they are localized in the body, are usually related indirectly to anger or fear and most certainly are related in a more direct way to pain. Misdirected or suppressed anger, repressed or excessive fear and chronic pain are all indications of imbalance in the first chakra of your physical body."[14]

When anger or fear is present, people may not be capable of deep or unconditional love for others; the heart center, which is an important energy hub within the body, may not function properly. As the Buddha so insightfully said, "In a controversy, the instant we feel anger we have already ceased striving for the truth and have begun striving for ourselves."[15] In time, this can lead to all sorts of potential health issues—physical, as well as emotional, mental, and spiritual.

If you are not in control of your ego mentally and emotionally, you may find yourself feeling separate from others. Or you may find that people are attracted to you from what they lack and for what you have to offer materially. Conversely, others may find it difficult to connect or develop intimacy with a big-ego personality type. In any of these cases, you may have less fulfilling relationships. One cannot have an open heart and an open mind toward others when patterns of anger, fear, or other ego traits take up so much space within.

So whether we are repressing anger and pushing others away or outwardly stamping our own personality on others,

*Principle Two: Thoughts and Emotions Are "Alive"*

the result is the same—we begin to isolate ourselves from others. The problem with all these mental patterns is that as human beings *we need connections* with other people and with a higher power to be healthy and fulfilled. In our natural state, as spiritual energy, we are already connected with each other by our minds. It is an illusion for any person to try to be an island unto him- or herself.

From my own experiences, I know that when anger sets in or when emotional troubles in my personality dominate my thoughts, the connection I feel with my Higher Source moves away. Or, more accurately, it is *me* that moves away—that inner power from the light is always there. When the personality takes over and the ego is in charge, communication with our higher self is more challenging. Perhaps this is why one acronym for ego is "Easing God Out."

To be fair, an ego is necessary for survival in most cultures on this planet. Often, though, our ego dominates our thoughts and leads to separation from our higher light as well as from others with whom we desire relations. Herein are the paradox and the delicate balance we tread each day of our lives.

## The Luminous Body

For the purposes of this material, I am referring to the "etheric body," or "etheric field," as the part of the aura that is closest to our physical body—the invisible field of energy that exists just above and all around the physical body. The etheric body is connected to our physical body and also acts as a bridge for spiritual energy to travel back and forth between worlds.

If there is a physical problem in one's body, it can be reflected and felt in one's etheric body. In the same way, an imbalance corrected by a surgeon in the physical body then shows up corrected in the etheric field. Likewise, healing energy can be administered by those who can hold God's light to correct imbalances in the etheric field. This energetic healing in turn can help correct ailments in the physical body.

This is why energy healing can work to help heal a variety of illnesses, both physical and emotional. From my experience, I have seen others healed from back pain, fluid imbalances in the brain, cancer, and emotional issues, and those in hospice actually transition to heaven as a result of now being free to move on. It is not a substitute for modern medicine, but sometimes there are answers right in front of us if we will recognize that we are beings of energy and can respond to a variety of healing methods.

After recovering from my cancer treatments, when I knew there was nothing else the Western doctors could do for me, I sought out a spiritual healer. My feeling was that I wanted to try anything that could tip the odds of survival in my favor. Although there were no remaining signs of my cancer, I knew that if it returned the chances of curing it were minimal. I had no particular beliefs either pro or con about alternative healing methods at that time in my life, but I understood there was little risk in trying something different.

Some might imagine that a person in the "alternative" healing field would seem different from the more traditional medical professionals. Yet when I met the healer for the first time, he looked like any common man you might bump into in the street; he was wearing jeans and a long sleeve dress shirt, and had an accent and long hair. He was a nice man, but he exhibited no particular expertise that I could recognize, nor did he wish to engage in deep conversation.

Once he began putting his hands around me, however, my body and, in fact, the whole room heated up with energy. It was so hot I was sweating, and it was all from this healer's hands! Soon enough, I felt as though I was going to fall asleep—and I almost did. When he removed his hands from my back, the heat fell away and I regained my sense of clarity. Any skepticism I had previously had as to whether this experience could be real quickly vanished as I came out of what felt like a light altered state. The experience had been warm and comfortable, and I knew something had happened, but there was no way to measure the results. Certainly, I was glad to have added this to my list of healing treatments, and emotionally it felt right to have experienced what may have been love from the Creator. I have since learned that spiritual healers as well as spiritual mediums have an understanding of how energy works and are more awakened to what our reality is than most of us.

Emotionally, many of us hold on to guilt, shame, heartache, and/or betrayal and allow these feelings to settle within us rather than working to resolve them. Yet these emotions tell us we are sensitive, that is, human, and each of these emotional feelings *can teach us something,* so it is important not to stuff them. Releasing repressed energy can help to restore balance to our aura. It can take the form of an emotional release, or this energy can be balanced by someone who understands how the energy flow works around and within the body.

Heartache as an emotion, for example, can lead to physical heart problems. Our heart center is vital to our survival both physically (energetically) and emotionally; they are connected. We often see that after a long marriage of forty or fifty years, when one spouse dies the other shortly follows suit. This is not just a coincidence—heartache can take its toll just like any other physical ailment.

Resentment is particularly troublesome, as it may not be as obvious a problem as anger or fear, yet it can cause as much illness as any other repressed emotion. Resentment can seek roots within the human body and ultimately short-circuit the natural flow of the body's energy patterns. This can result in a loss of power to a particular place in the physical body, which is what Rosalyn Bruyere was referring to with regard to power imbalances.

For example, when stuck emotions short-circuit the natural flow of power to areas such as the kidneys, stomach, lungs, or nervous system, the energy flow is interrupted. Then potential illnesses such as kidney cancer, ulcers, asthma, and nerve disorders can take hold. In contrast, when we allow stuck energy to be released, we can return to health and well-being again. A quote from *The Daily Om* captures this well: "Emotionally, we take flight when the strength of our passion exceeds the strength of our blockages; the floodgates open and we are free to feel fully!"[16]

I have many financial planning clients who are well into their retirement, and I observe their behavior. Mostly this is in their interest to make sure they are following my direction and avoiding any planning mistakes. Still, I have seen nervous people with overactive personalities over a period of many years burn out; they become predisposed to disorders, from hand tremors to headaches. Like anything else, your nervous system will suffer wear and tear from your emotional state; it can lead to potential physical illness.

## *Fear as an Emotion*

Many of us hold on to our fears too tightly. Emotionally, we are creatures of habit, and we believe we are serving ourselves by attending to our notions of what is right for us. In fact, though, we are strengthening our fears by attending to these false beliefs and mental patterns; it is said that whatever we put our attention on grows. Many times I have fought with friends over trivial matters to protect my position just to keep myself

## Principle Two: Thoughts and Emotions Are "Alive"

from changing or trying new things. However, when we do this, we may lose out on something that may be quite beneficial, fun, and/or growth producing for us.

Let me give you an example. My father practically brainwashed me into believing that if I ever snow skied I would break a leg. As a result, since I owned my own business and was worried about who would take care of things if something happened to me, I was pretty fixed to never go skiing. Then came a huge snowstorm, and a very persuasive friend convinced me to give it a go. I took the chairlift to the top of a mountain in Vermont, and it was so high in the sky that I watched my life pass before me as the cars at the bottom of the mountain were barely visible.

When I got to the peak, it was similar to standing on top of a very tall building and looking down at people, who look like dots in the street. The cold, blustery wind began shearing off my skin, and at some point I realized I had to get down the mountain and began skiing and tumbling down it, not very gracefully, to be sure. Instead of quitting, though, I put other people's opinions, including my father's, to the side, persevered, and years later I am now an accomplished skier—and I love the sport! I have learned that in our approach to life's challenges, it is our flexible attitude and having an open mind that leads to intended results.

We all have fears, and they may be different for each of us. It might be fear of being our true selves, fear of not being loved, fear of being perceived as weak, fear of being taken advantage of, fear of losing control, fear of not being enough, fear of not having enough, fear of having too much, fear of being last, fear of being late, fear of being alone, fear of loss, fear due to phobias, fear of other people . . . and on and on it goes. Perhaps you can think of others that are personal to you.

It is reasonable to have some fears and concerns; this can

keep us mentally alert, which reduces errors. However, it can be taken too far, keeping us from seeing the whole picture right in front of us. Often, people are too rigid in their mental patterns, and if they just looked a little to the left or a little to the right, it would lead to a very different decision-making process. We too easily dismiss others' points of view, when the truth is that they are just as connected as we are to divine influences, and there is as much validity to their thoughts and feelings as ours. Being receptive to what they have to say and open to what the world throws at our doorstep can be powerful.

Ideally, our relationships with others should be about listening to each other and being willing to learn from one another, yet too often my listening was closed down and it made me resistant to change. Over time, as I became less fearful, I became more open to possibility. Being discerning is good, but the more amenable we are to another's point of view, the more new opportunities may reveal themselves. When we are less fearful, we become more receptive to listening because we are not focused on defending ourselves. It is a sign of growth when we have a mind quiet enough to listen.

### Evolving beyond Fear to Love and Gratitude

There is a fear about survival that has been built into humanity over thousands of years. So whether it is real or perceived as real, fear is likely ingrained into our DNA and has worked as a useful survival mechanism as we have evolved throughout history. However, in a civilized society, fear only works to obstruct our emotions. When we are in a state of fear, we may act out behaviors that we ultimately regret. Furthermore, when fear is present it tends to override most other thoughts and higher emotions. We may become more like an animal fighting for our basic needs, even if it is likely only a perceived need.

*Principle Two: Thoughts and Emotions Are "Alive"*

Interestingly, the fears discussed in this chapter apply not only to each of us individually but also to countries and governments. Although we are at the top of the food chain, our natural instincts, which have helped us survive for so long, now prevent us as a civilization from uniting and moving forward in peace and brotherhood. The constant warring among groups and nations reflects a survivalist mentality that has no authentic place anymore. The destructive weapons the military uses for war are more powerful too.

War, famine, economic competition, and planetary resources to support a growing global population may threaten our survival because of our inability across the globe to get along with one another. Mother Earth may be telling us to change the path we are on through the disrupting weather patterns, violent storms, and rising water levels on our shores.

Oddly enough, fear can also unify us in a strange way, whether as individuals or as nations. If you think of one word that may describe a common behavior that friends, coworkers, family, acquaintances, strangers, people in the news, people you know, and those you don't, it's probably *fear*. Think, for example, of how fear of "the enemy" united both people in the United States and many citizens of other Western countries after the vicious attacks of September 11, 2001. In one form or another fear is widespread and does not discriminate between rich and poor, or First World and Third World nations, and so on.

Fear is an emotion, and so logic does not act as a pacifier to it. You can talk and talk until you are blue in the face with people who are living in fear, and it will not change them. Often, they do not know they are living in fear; their behavior has become quite natural for them. Says martial artist Bruce Lee, "It is only when we are walking about the Earth that we feel separate and different from each other. It is we who make ourselves feel this way as we are driven by fear and ego. Under heaven there is but one family. It just so happens people are different."[17]

So, what may be a prescription to move beyond our fears? The answer is to come from love and gratitude, which make it difficult for fear to take hold. Love is the most "vibrant" of all the emotions, and it can take many forms. And when one has gratitude, it may offset fear in the same way as having an optimistic viewpoint changes one's perspective from looking at a glass as being half empty to seeing it as half full. In essence, if we change our mental attitude, we change our emotional response. I know, as I have seen this work in myself and have witnessed it in others. Sometimes, because of our fear, a simple solution is often overlooked even though it is right in front of us.

Some of the exercises practiced in Circle work are designed to expand our energy vibration based on love. Our resultant thought patterns and the intention we have to help another human being are this same vibration. Eventually, the service work some people choose to do with others outside the Circle follows the same pattern. By helping to lift and assist others, in turn it lifts them to a higher vibration.

Fear is one obstacle that prevents most of us from reaching our true capabilities and ascending higher on our path. The meditations and exercises in a Circle compel you to look within and face your fears, which is perhaps the greatest benefit of working in this capacity. Out in the world, most people are so attentive to everything going on around them that there is little time to focus within.

Through the spiritual exercises and meditations, my mind shifted as my emotional self became lighter. This enabled me to vibrate my energy at a higher level and eventually communicate with those in heaven. Some of the lessons and information contained in this book are a result of collaboration with those in the spiritual dimensions. The purpose for anyone who

## Principle Two: Thoughts and Emotions Are "Alive"

is able to connect in this way is to share this knowledge so we can all move forward as a civilization.

It took me almost losing my life to figure out that the real secrets reside within us. I had to learn to take ownership of my life. I finally realized that if I did not change my attitudes and beliefs, nothing in my outer world would change. You, too, can take control of your thought patterns and emotions, and thus have the opportunity to manifest something different for yourself. This pays more dividends than any financial advice I have ever given my clients.

Edgar Cayce, in his "Reading 3253-2," captures the power of these efforts to take responsibility for our lives:

> For the greater individual is the one who is the servant of all. And to conquer self is greater than taking many cities. For, here ye may find humbleness as against that which cries out for expression, and the feeling of not being appreciated. Express it more in the greater amount of love upon those who may be aided through thy effort. For, remember, man looks upon the things of the day but God looks upon the heart.[18]

In Circle, I have witnessed communications from those who have passed over into heaven, and it has been said that we as human beings should cherish the time we have here as a gift. We should learn to experience all the emotions of grief, anger, loss, and fear, then release them so that we can experience joy, love, and peace, and live life to its fullest. ஃ *From grief we then appreciate joy; from anger we then appreciate happiness; from loss we then appreciate gain; from fear we then appreciate love; from violence we then appreciate peace.* ஃ

In essence, we have the potential to shift and grow with the release of our emotional baggage. Otherwise, the progression we have explored of our thoughts leading to our feelings, then to our emotions, and finally to taking on real "form" will result in undesirable manifestations that inhibit our growth rather than promote it. However, once we let go of what no longer serves us and begin this shift, life is never again the same. We may begin tapping into the same higher power and energy that surrounds us all, which has love as its essence. We begin to realize that there is nothing to fear and everything to gain.

CHAPTER 6

# PRINCIPLE THREE:
# THE POWER OF UNITY

> *All things appear and disappear because of the concurrence of causes and conditions. Nothing ever exists entirely alone; everything is in relation to everything else.*
>
> —Buddha, thinkexist.com

If we take water and heat, two substances not normally found together, and mix them, we have one of the most powerful energies on Earth—steam! This is the same energy used to propel jet fighters off the short runways of aircraft carriers. And, if we can find a way to unite the people of this planet instead of focusing on our differences, we will be able combine our energy to move civilization a huge leap forward.

While it is our God-given right to have free will and make choices, every decision by each of us has consequences not only for ourselves but for others. We are connected to each other in ways most of us have yet to discover. If we consider the environment, for example, we are now seeing this process unfold from our choices as a society or as a nation and the world in general. And, many of us can feel it. The Earth's response to us is her shifting of her own energy ever so slightly as her vibration speeds up, and this change in vibration affects all of us.[1] We are also seeing physical shifts, such as in the tectonic plates below the Pacific Ocean, and what appears to be an increase in natural disasters, as well as the melting of the polar ice caps.

Sometimes truth is stranger than fiction. In the movie *The Matrix*, we learn how those in what is referred to as the "Matrix" have no idea that they are living in a computer program and that the real world actually resides somewhere else. Just a few people in the movie are able to escape and make it outside of the Matrix and see the world as it truly exists.[2]

Today most people in our world, regardless of intelligence, social status, religion, or country, are living in a type of matrix. They are on automatic, without a thought or regard for the possibility of life beyond death or why they are here in the first place. The truth is that *we are spirits in human form, not humans that become spirits, and we each have a specific purpose to fulfill in our time on this planet that ultimately benefits all.*

Many of us are indifferent to or hold little compassion for others. If people really believed in the interconnectedness that ties us together—that we are all the same without our flesh on—the separation they feel would no longer exist.

Too often, for economic reasons countries look the other way when governments persecute their own people, at times slaughtering the innocent for reasons most cannot comprehend. For the persecutors, it is always fear on some level that is driving this behavior. For the victims, the fear of death is greater than anything else and a motivator to conform even if their civil rights or freedom is lost. For those observing, the attitude usually is that "it is better to let someone else's problems be theirs, not mine." Yet, for the world to *evolve*, we all need to be *involved*.

World War II was practically an apocalypse, with tens of millions killed either in battle or in labor camps. This shocking death toll should have put an end to all wars among humanity, yet this is obviously not the case. We as a civilization are not learning our lessons from history. The weapons have changed, but the struggles and the fears among the human race have not. If it were up to the Universal Intelligence surrounding us and the beings who guide us, war and slaughter would not be our path. But until people understand why they are here and their attitudes toward themselves and others change, condemnation and disrespect for life will not change. If we as a species were more heart based with our decisions, war would be less likely.

All of us can connect with a unified vision if we can end war and lower our weapons long enough to permit trust between nations to develop. The Olympics seem to be the only time that all nations from around the globe can be together without turmoil. All people matter, and all governments need to foster cooperation with each other for harmony to exist. Chaos in one region of our planet, with its destabilizing energy pattern, is not in the interest of those trying to promote partnerships with one another.

## *One Earth, One Voice*

The diversity in cultures throughout the world has kept societies fragmented from one another until now. Technology has the people of India working as support teams for American companies on a daily basis. Terrorist groups have used technology for recruiting potential members from faraway lands. People go on the Internet and scan through hundreds of pictures to meet potential mates from throughout the world. Through technology the world is getting smaller all the time.

Our cell phones, e-mails, faxes, Skype, and FaceTime make even our friends who might be three thousand miles away feel as if they are in the room next door. No longer will small voices in distant places remain silent. More are being heard worldwide now because of technology, and in time all will have the opportunity to speak with their own voices and be listened to by a world audience.

The Middle East is an example of where through modern technology we can literally see the world changing right before our eyes. It was "business as usual" for many dictatorships until computers, cell phones, and the Internet raised awareness. Now that information has become more widely available, the common people of dictatorships and oppressed nations have become no longer so invisible; they have become potentially empowered humans. Their way of life has ceased to be fulfilling, and they are risking their lives for freedom—and the world is watching.

The speed of communication and the accessibility to information is leveling the playing field not only in business and economics, but also socially. More than just freedom, a change in awareness is occurring in the world like never before.

As a world community, we have become intolerant of rogue nations such as Iran and North Korea, with their military threats toward others and their suppression of human rights. Ultimately, as a world community, we will need to act in a unified way as one voice rather than having the same countries acting as policemen all the time. As the world gets smaller, countries will become neighborhoods. If you live in a "bad" neighborhood, with enough effort it can be changed. If it cannot be saved, then it becomes isolated and eventually choked off until it dies. Then a cycle of new life begins again in place of the old.

Time is speeding up as the days blend into weeks and years, as technology moves our civilization forward at a pace beyond what anybody could have imagined even thirty years ago. The human race has mastered planet Earth and its physical domain. Unfortunately, it is behind spiritually and emotionally, and lacks the maturity at this time to safely guide itself through Earth's dwindling resources and the potentially all-encompassing destructive technologies of war. We have not been responsible stewards, and this needs to change.

Unity may sound utopian but, like it or not, we are moving as a civilization toward this goal. Cooperation and peace are necessary to keep us from self-destructing. The technology in weapons has become far too advanced and may soon threaten our existence.

❧ *The lives we lead, the planet we live on, and the choices we make as a civilization are all a learning exercise—in the progression of our evolution as people and the evolution of our souls.* ❧ Every choice our country or other nations make potentially can have an impact on something else down the line. In heaven's eyes, the world we live in is essentially a test tube for all of us, and over time it is getting smaller.

Dr. Ernest Holmes concisely captures the essence of our individual responsibility toward creating a unified, peaceful world in the following quote:

> If we would promote the idea of peace in the world, we must begin with our own individual consciousness. . . . The mind that is always confused and distraught is not at peace; the mind that is continuously upset and agitated by the little, petty things of life is not at peace; it is at war with itself. It is only when individual mind ceases combating itself that it will stop combating others.[3]

## The Reality of Our Life

As we begin to understand that all life has purpose and a deeper meaning, more subtle things begin to appear. I cannot remember earlier in my youth ever looking at a flower, animals, or a place in nature and appreciating its beauty as I do today. Fortunately, the same can be said for my tolerance of other people who are different from me. Before my Circle work this was not always the case, as I tended to focus on *differences* between myself and others rather than on *similarities*.

Some of you may never be able to think of yourself as being similar to others who are different. You may be thinking, "This just isn't me." Well, it wasn't me either only a few years ago. When you recognize that your life is connected with many others and know that existence is continuous, your heart opens quite naturally. This does not, however, mean that you become weak—not at all—just more aware. You may gain a deeper perspective and appreciation of where you fit in.

Try engaging someone who seems very different from you and see if you can find a similarity and something you share in common. You can take baby steps at first. This would be easier than waiting for a crisis to cross your path, resulting in hardship that raises your awareness and forces changes in your thinking. Too often, people need to experience a tragedy before they shift their awareness or change their attitudes, yet we can be proactive about this instead. I realize that you may be a person who needs to learn through your own experiences, and that is fine. Through sharing my story, I simply hope to lessen the blow or help you avoid it all together.

If you do not yet know what purpose you have or specific role you are to play in life, just being present and having knowledge that your life here is not an accident gives you importance. Even if your parents told you that you were an accident or that you were not wanted, you are here by choice and your decision to incarnate from the other side. Everything is interconnected, so your place has meaning no matter how much you fight or resist this basic premise of your existence. The reality of flesh is tangible for each of us and so we can

## Principle Three: The Power of Unity

relate to it; however, our soul, or spiritual nature, is somewhat intangible and thus harder to grasp.

᭢ *Our real form of being, when not in our physical body, is that of pure consciousness—we are beings of light energy as a thought form. This is why having a physical body and experiencing this reality is a gift.* ᭢ The sensations of touch and taste are unique to the human body and this environment. So is the ability to speak and use the power of the word as a means of communication, as are the multitude of lessons for our own personal growth and experience in this fast-paced emotional and physical environment we presently call home.

### Religion

The question of whether one considers oneself to be "religious" is a sensitive topic, as this form of identity means so much to people and resonates to the core of their belief systems. If you listen closely, many will often define themselves by their particular religion and then define others who do not share the same religious beliefs as separate from them. This narrows one's perspective of reality and closes down thinking, resulting in one becoming the opposite of open-minded.

Unfortunately, throughout history this behavior has repeated itself and has developed into an "us versus them" mentality. Most conflicts in our history have had their roots based in religious ideals. Even in the modern world, this still goes on in many areas of the globe. Religion can be a positive force in one's life, especially if it is heart based, but if it is based only on formal dogma, it can create division rather than unity. It must be seen as a method for speaking to your Maker, your Source, rather than as an element for defining who you are.

Religion can bring you closer to Spirit through prayer; however, it is important to note that the specific customs in each religion are *man-made* rather than created by God, which causes them to appear distinct from each other. However, if you look at the essence of all faiths, you will probably find more similarities than differences. We are meant to be one tribe—if religion was something God had created, there might be only one.

We have found many ways to honor and speak to God in community. As a young race, many thousands of years ago, people may have created different forms of religions and rituals to find ways to respect and express devotion to what they believed was their Maker. And to find ways to perhaps appease their gods and bring people together. Religion, when used properly, provides us a way to honor our Creator and what is good in life, as well as to give thanks. Unfortunately, it is sometimes misused to create divisiveness and to take people away from their true spiritual paths as individuals and as a collective.

The truth is that no religion has the exclusive formula for having a relationship with Spirit—there is no one right way to speak to our Creator. Neither is there a "wrong" way. God is love, and this has no religious boundaries. God is everywhere and is everything. All of us have a piece of God in us. We are all from the same source, and after this physical existence we will return to this source together.

When we understand how similar we are to each other and that we can have a personal relationship with our Maker, the better we will all be. There may be rules and guidelines we can gain from various cultures and traditions, but in reality our relationship with God is individual. Many fear that they won't be accepted by God and so they follow religious prescriptions for behavior like a checklist, thinking, *If I say this or do that, I will be given the keys to the kingdom. I am right for believing and doing it this way, and others who do not are sinful.* This plants the seeds for conflict.

## Principle Three: The Power of Unity

Adherents to the major religions often set up competition about who is right. As with children fighting for their parents' attention, an escalation of rivalry can lead to violence. Children can harbor ill will for life if they feel that their parents loved the other sibling more, even if it is only a perception and not truth. Likewise, when the rivalry is for God's love and attention, people cannot fathom that there is enough of either to go around. But the reality is that to the Creator, the soul of one person is as important as that of another. Instead, with their misperceptions, people fight wars and kill each other to take the favored spot. This is an illusion—there is no chosen spot to be taken, as we are each inhabited by a soul that is equal to the Source in heaven.

The reality is that God loves *all* its children and cannot possibly ever choose one religion over another. You are born into your circumstances for your soul's reasons rather than to gain favor in God's eyes. The Great Spirit put you on this Earth for a creative purpose, and your soul's journey is unique. God would never support the killing or destruction of another human being in its name. This is the universal lesson we must learn.

Love is universal and is what will bring you closer to the Source, and it does not have to be only for another human being—it is for *all* of life, in both the physical and nonphysical dimensions. Love raises your vibration, which opens your heart and builds a bridge to connect with energy beyond the physical world. Hate, anger, and violence lower your vibration and distance you from the Creator. There is nothing wrong with having emotions appropriate to your situation; that is part of being human. Still, there is no need to dwell on negative or nonproductive emotions as pervasive traits through your choices. You can shift the designation of yourself as being an angry person to "I feel angry in this particular moment, and my anger is telling me something." It is always going to be your choice—you decide what is in your heart.

You can also shift your perspective about other people being in competition with you. It seems to be a human trait to view others as competing for food, love, money, and general resources. When in our evolutionary process we were living on the level of survival, this internal sense of competitiveness served us well as a species, as I have mentioned. However, as we enter a more conscious and enlightened age, collaboration is more important than competitive edge. Collaboration creates energy. If people share their resources with each other, there could potentially be twice as much available. Even if you are not ready for this way of looking at things, remember that it takes less energy to love your neighbor than to find ways to compete with him or her.

With the proliferation of nuclear weapons, the global population on the rise, and increasing limits on our natural resources, the time is now for us to become more responsible and be aware of our choices. Scarcity can be a state of mind that leads to fear and competition, which leads to a "hoarding" mentality. The result of this thinking is conflict and all sorts of justifications for bad behavior, which in turn blocks energy and the ability for all of us to have what we need. Everyone matters and deserves a good life. You are important, and you can learn to have what you want, know what you need, and share with others without taking anything away from what you—or they—deserve. In fact, you may have less stress and more joy in what you do have if you are not afraid of losing it or having too little.

This leads us back to the question of religion. In its highest form, religion teaches respect for other people and love for family and self, honors the Creator, and assists in bringing its members closer to God. If it is heart based, it will be God based.

*Principle Three: The Power of Unity*

However, the believer must be discerning. It is not God's will that religion be used as an excuse for a means to an end against others. If a religious leader is trying to misuse religion to direct and control people's behavior in ways that are un-God-like, this is likely to be a *human* endeavor rather than divinely inspired. God does not need money or power in the ways that humanity lusts for it. Religious leaders have human frailty and therefore should not be empowered to be more than they are—we should not glorify them and give them authority that belongs to God alone. It is up to the faithful to be willing to speak out against abuse and to assure that their messages are pure and their behaviors are consistent with God's love. It is up to the faithful to shine a light on misuse, misdirection, and religious manipulation. Earth's history shows this harmful pattern to be a never-ending cycle, and it is time for it to stop.

### History Repeats Itself

While God, the angels, and the universe will not force us to change, the choices we have made to this point are making change necessary for the continuation of life on our planet. We must learn to cooperate before there is a tragedy. One message I have received several times from my guides in heaven is:
↬ *Our survival as a world community going forward is going to require cooperation. There will be coming Earth changes, as well as food-supply and energy shortages that will require the world's inhabitants to rely on each other.* ↫

Even if you question this message, this last sentence reveals what is ultimately going to be unavoidable—we have to work together for survival. If we embrace these challenges and learn to see each other as equals on this journey called "human," we will be better able to weather them. We are not meant to suffer or be punished. We are meant to evolve as *one people*.

Cooperation requires a mentality of love, equality, and concern for others rather than wanting everything for oneself. We need to learn to share resources if we are to ever live in true peace.

## Politics

I have heard people say, "I don't believe in politics," as if we can somehow make ourselves immune. The reality is, if you live on Earth, you are affected by politics. No matter how many times you shut off the television or avoid your computer, there is still a physical world surrounding you with people making decisions that you may never understand. If we as a society allow killing, discrimination, domination, mistreatment, and withholding of freedoms from one another anywhere, we are inhibiting the primary reason for our incarnation on this planet, which is to fulfill our divine paths. We as people need to understand who we are—that we are more than just a reflection in the mirror each day. We also need to know that what happens in the world impacts every soul.

Another message I am continually receiving from those in heaven is this: *The killing or taking of what others have for our own benefit must stop. Leaders using fear as a control mechanism and countries showing overpowering aggression to their people as well as to their neighbors must cease. Continuing this behavior will have consequences not only now but in generations that follow. Those who are responsible for making these decisions will answer to a higher power when they eventually cross over to the other side at death. It is this simple.*

Herein is the dilemma: As we make choices that we feel are best for each of us, and for our survival in business or as a nation, not enough thought is given to our neighbors and to others living in faraway lands or even to other possible future realities if we do not make the right choices now.

## Principle Three: The Power of Unity

Politics, which should be the governance of people for the benefit of civilization, has too many conflicts of interest. The desire for wealth and the underlying competition for dominance is the opposite of the cooperative, collaborative planet God intended for us.

Businesses as well as governments are political, with special-interest groups and conflicts of interest. To illustrate: In business, there is a natural conflict of interest that occurs between the management of a public company and its shareholders. It is called the "agency" problem.[4] The management wants to maximize their income, and often it is at the expense of shareholders, who want to maximize their wealth. The more the management is paid—and sometimes it can be large amounts—less remains for the company's net profit that flows to the shareholders.

While it is true that corporations have helped to make America powerful, it is also true that the large corporation has other motivations and agendas that may not be in congruence with the citizens of the planet. After all, the primary motive in business is profits. Sadly, the environment, pollution, unemployment, and unfair competition are some of the many areas that are potentially in direct conflict with corporate profitability.

Like in business, governments often have conflicts with their constituents. We find it worse in some political systems than in others, but conflicts still exist. A politician attaining a high level of office must owe favors and make deals with folks who helped him attain office. Once elected, the politician may make decisions favoring those political forces that help him maintain his power base rather than decisions that are best for all. Sure, there will be decisions that help the general populace, but there are still too many deals behind closed doors helping the few special interests.

We find this to be true not only in the United States but in other governments of the world. Some political systems are dictatorial, as power is passed forward by decree or bloodline. These systems will come under pressure as the world continues developing and information dissemination through technology levels the playing field between those in power and everyone else.

## Hope Comes with Changing Vibration

I am here to tell you that there is hope! As the coming changes in the Earth's vibration begin taking hold, if a politician flies on a carpet of deception, the public will know it. In time, and especially with a commitment to developing other senses beyond our physical ones, it will become easier to understand other people with our own intuition and to know within ourself what resonates as feeling right. Leaders will come to believe that what is best for the people will also be best for themselves, as our forefathers understood. There will be no double standards for the few at the top.

We should not, ourselves, stand in judgment—we need to remember to leave that to God and to not hold accountable individuals who have no responsibility for the actions of a few. We cannot condemn entire nations; it is people who kill other people, not countries. Individual souls are judged on their merits by their Creator, not upon nationality in a physical incarnation. Many people still have not forgiven the Germans for World War II. However, it was the Nazi Party, not the entire population of Germany, that was responsible for the atrocities that occurred during that war. There were obviously a lot of people who caused great harm, but this certainly was not all Germans.

The same can be said today with Iran and many other countries on any given day. The world is in chaos in ways that may not always appear on the news. There may be people in a position of power running policy that will fly under the radar for a period of time. But eventually, as we are in the Information Age, knowledge is transmitted for the world to see in a mere matter of seconds. All nations need to act in unison to overcome these evils before they are released on others. When we embrace this new way of looking at the world, the ability for each of us to find love and compassion for one another without judgment will enable harmony and peace to take hold in a way this world has never seen.

## *Economics*

The views I traditionally held before my engagement with Circle work are those of an American capitalist, so the next paragraphs are truly different from the medicine I was raised on. My spiritual path and the messages received from Spirit have shown me what we need, which is to bring understanding and ultimate prosperity to all. My personal view of prosperity has changed. If some are wealthy but others do not have their basic needs met, this is not prosperity. Moving forward as a society and a civilization, we must make greater efforts to help people with their basic needs. This will make it possible for more of humanity to make a contribution to the whole.

There are three major socioeconomic models, a brief description of which follows. None is perfect, and each has costs and benefits. Looking at them from a spiritual perspective offers other possible solutions to challenges in the years ahead.

### *Communism*

Communism may provide more resources than the other two economic models for the basic needs of its citizens, such as food, shelter, education, and health care. We see this type of economic and political model operating in China. However, it lacks the freedoms that are required to foster creativity, personal growth, imagination, and social awareness, which are some of the basic areas that we embrace as part of our spiritual growth and expansion of consciousness in a free society. Ultimately, in a communistic system many will not be able to evolve and expand their own development and will lack inner fulfillment. It stifles the human condition and a sense of individuality.

*Capitalism*

In the United States capitalism certainly rewards creativity and those who work hard to get ahead in life with prosperity; we may call it a system of merit. However, not everyone has the same opportunity to create, receive a good education, receive the same benefits, and have the same work opportunities or living standards, especially if they do not have enough food to eat or a roof over their heads. Due to these fundamental inequalities, many will not be able to create, contribute, and evolve as others in this society.

In the name of progress, capitalism is an economic model that focuses mainly on big business and productivity at a potential cost to the "little guy." It is no secret that companies will hire and fire at will, saving their own hide to maximize the bottom line. Capitalism is a system of great rewards, but too many are left as "road kill" watching from the sidelines.

*Socialism*

The third social and economic model is democratic socialism, which is perhaps a midpoint between communism and capitalism. It represents cooperative management of essential resources needed for maintaining economic production. An example is Europe, where the basic health care and retirement needs of citizens are provided for; there is opportunity for business creativity; and the society is still an open one for ideas, news, writing, and speech. Freedom is a basic component, and, as such, the opportunity for one to experience personal growth and an expansion of awareness is intact.

However, not all is perfect with this system either. Taxes can potentially be greater to support the resources provided to its citizens. Also, there may be less incentive to do more and take risks compared to the merit system under capitalism. Yet this model offers everyone a fair opportunity so all people may develop their gifts and contribute in some way.

## *In the Age of Spiritual Advancement*

There is not "one" of these socioeconomic models that works best above all others. Each has positive and negative attributes. Capitalism has the most freedoms, socialism has its citizens share economic services, and communism sees that all its citizens have their basic needs met, such as food and a roof over their heads. Still, within each system there remain imbalances with haves and have-nots.

So what might be the most viable economic model for today's world? As a man who has spent his prespiritual awakening and postspiritual awakening in the field of finance, I have some vision of what might work. I may even be receiving this vision from across the veil and can understand it because of my experiences.

Ideally, this type of system starts with a fair economic model and an open political system that supports freedom of expression for its citizens. Rather than changing the US system, if we could take capitalism and *require* that a larger percentage of government or corporate revenues be driven into specific socioeconomic domestic programs (not entitlements), it might be a better model than what is currently in place. This plan requires not necessarily increasing government but rather redirecting how the money is spent. Perhaps finding new ways to incentivize more donations from the haves to the have-nots is a part of the solution.

This ideal system also stresses good family values and an opportunity for all to receive a decent education, not just people who can happen to afford one. There would be more cooperation within and among each nation's citizens; the idea of getting ahead at all costs would be eliminated rather than rewarded. There would be a system in place besides tax deductions that would require or reward large corporate entities for sharing their wealth.

A system that creates greater incentives than what exists now is necessary to persuade the elite to share with those in need. It cannot always be about who has the most money, "toys," and material objects, which are fleeting anyway. Yet when people are successful financially at the top of the food chain, they often fear change—it is an unknown, and some may feel safer boxing themselves in rather than facing a modification.

What is truly important, though, is to feel life on a heart level. Otherwise, there is no telling what sort of harsh experiences may find a way to our doorstep to equalize this situation. This would not be a punishment, but rather a natural balancing so more people have the opportunity to experience a full life. Economic downshifts from the top, for example, are ways to wake people up to their values.

As time elapses and the world's financial problems potentially become more severe, the solutions stated here may become more obvious to others on a larger scale. Already it appears that the Western economic models in America and parts of Europe are collapsing under their own weight, with

## Principle Three: The Power of Unity

trillions in debt. We may come to see that money may not be the only means of value to transfer for goods and services. In time, other forms of compensation may become necessary for payment and reward.

Ultimately, we are here for learning, evolving, and expanding ourselves through our experiences and the lessons that are put before us. Eliminating poverty and hunger and providing shelter create a minimum baseline for all who are less fortunate. It enables everyone to have a chance at life. It enables all to be less focused on survival and therefore more likely to make a contribution to others and our planet.

If we remain asleep and too set in our way, we will face many challenges ahead. Compassion is currently one of the most important spiritual lessons to learn for the citizens of Earth. People need to see and respond to the struggles of others as well as to their own. There is a tremendous amount of wasted energy spent on trying to step over each other from day to day. If we change some of these patterns in society, its members will have more freedom to produce, create, and live freely.

There are other ways to measure wealth that we need to explore as a people and a civilization. We were not put here for competition to see who can obtain the most possessions. Granted, there are lessons to be learned in the human experience of creating riches and reaching a true abundance consciousness in the struggle of overcoming poverty. The larger economic systems now in place have often focused our attention on the less important material aspects of life.

Right now there are too many interest groups with their hand in the cookie jar as they throw their weight behind a political candidate to force change that favors them. We cannot keep changing policies every four years depending on which party wins office. Otherwise, in time, if we cannot get our finances in check, another economic model or format may take place as our financial imbalances widen. The deeper the separation between the haves and the have-nots, the riskier it is for politicians to stay the course. Currently, this gap is widening and pointing to change in many areas both in the United States and abroad.

From a spiritual perspective, this change is welcome. When those at the socioeconomic bottom worry less about their basic needs, they will have more possibilities for developing themselves as human beings. In turn, this will lead people to focus on their hearts and minds, eventually turning their attention beyond their physical needs, and therefore making them more likely to make a contribution to others. Opportunities are then created for enrichment not just for a few, but for the whole.

## *Anyone Can Commune with Heaven*

Renowned scientist and inventor Albert Einstein's often-quoted wisdom may hold a key to our dilemma: "We cannot solve our problems with the same thinking we used when we created them."[5] What I am about to suggest may be a huge stretch for some to allow into their current mind-sets, but I believe there is great merit to it: let us look *beyond ourselves* to the guidance available to us from the spiritual plane of existence.

Those who have had near-death experiences or who are psychically developed have had the opportunity to sense these other realities. In actuality, we all possess the ability to sense beyond our normal, everyday, tangible world, as we likely visit other planes of existence every night during our sleep. We can also develop these abilities actively through such exercises and practices that I did in my work in Circle.

When I learned that I could connect with heaven and those in the nonphysical dimensions, my inquisitive nature took over. There were so many things I wanted to know

## Principle Three: The Power of Unity

about. I am certain I was like the proverbial toddler discovering language and the world for the first time, wondering, *What's this? How does this work?* And the crazy-making (for parents) word *Why?* Fortunately, our spirit guides expect and encourage this kind of curiosity.

When you connect with guides, ascended beings, and what I like to call "Source" or "Spirit," the questions and answers change. It is like being given the keys to the kingdom. You will be given answers that you can comprehend, and you may receive information that inspires you to think of the answer. Of course, we always have free will to make our own choices.

A word of caution here: it is important to note that if we are talking to loved ones who have crossed over, they may or may not know much more than we do. Human beings do not become instantly enlightened because they have left the physical plane. The process of enlightenment takes time on both sides of the veil.

As a way to begin exploring the idea that we all have the ability to communicate with and learn from those in the nonphysical dimensions, think about whether you have ever had contact with a deceased loved one during sleep. You wake up knowing you had a conversation with a friend or family member who has passed over, but upon awakening your rational mind takes over and you begin to dismiss the possibility that it was real. Likely it was genuine, yet perhaps only if the deceased person was "warning you" about something might you allow yourself to believe it. Otherwise, you might not give it much credence for fear of ridicule.

Since I started working with and practicing with my own psychic energies in Circle, I have had a number of dreams where deceased loved ones have visited with me. The talks are brief but always meaningful, with a message pertaining to something in my life. Usually it has been one of my grandparents—most commonly my grandmother, with whom I was closest while she was still alive on the physical plane. In these communications, she always offers me inspiration and support. Once she came to tell me that my mother would be all right after she was stricken with cancer. It was a difficult time for all of us, and Mom's disease ended up being a stage IV lung cancer that easily could have taken her life. However, she made it through, just as Grandma had predicted.

In another dream, my grandmother offered a message of encouragement relative to the difficult period I was experiencing in my marriage. We were going through a real rough patch, and this dose of inspiration from her gave me hope that things were going to work themselves out for the better. It was not a long dream, but one that seemed emotionally charged with love.

The dream took place in Grandma's kitchen; she had always been a good cook, so this seemed very apropos. This had been a comfortable place for me that held warm memories; I would sit still in this environment and listen to whatever Grandma had to say. She looked really good and healthy and was all smiles, and she was wearing one of her cooking aprons that I recognized—white with a red border. Her lips barely moved, but her thoughts resonated with me loudly and clearly. "Don't worry so much, dear; it will be all right," she communicated to me. Inspiration filled with loving support from the right person is sometimes all it takes to set things right.

We are all capable of dream communication during sleep. Dreaming is accessing the subconscious, which is the world just between our reality and heaven. And, since we all need to sleep, it is feasible to experience this. You only need to set the intention before bedtime and be open to possibility.

*Principle Three: The Power of Unity*

## *Issues to Contemplate*

Although a bit controversial, I have asked my guides about important issues that seem to divide us and separate us from each other. In the next sections are the answers I received about abortion, reincarnation, and suicide, and I acknowledge that they are based on my questions and thought processes. I do not claim to have all the answers. These were satisfying to me, and therefore I share them to help you form your own opinions on these subjects.

### *Abortion*

Beyond religion there are very few issues that are more divisive than abortion for human beings. This is a sensitive topic, with many people on both sides of the debate. Sometimes this discussion cannot be separated from religion, or it becomes the basis for definition or separation. So I asked Spirit about it and learned the following information that may be helpful in bringing people together on the issue.

Life is in existence in spiritual form before a baby is conceived, and life as spirit exists again after the physical body wears out. ᛦ *Spirit forms matter, not the other way around.* ᛦ

At conception, the soul with great anticipation sees an opportunity to be born into the physical universe. During pregnancy, this soul more and more begins attaching itself to the unborn fetus until birth, when both the soul (spiritual self) and the baby are born as one.

Therefore, if a pregnancy is terminated prematurely, it may be considered by some to be an ethical offense and disappointing, but it is not murder in the strict sense. The soul and the essence of what gives life to the physical child is not, and can never be, killed. In the case of abortion, for example, the soul simply waits for its next opportunity to incarnate. However, terminating a pregnancy before birth impedes the cycle of life that is in motion, and there can be physical and psychological implications experienced by the mother from making this decision. Thus, great care and sensitivity must be used when interfering with the laws of nature.

Spirit knows what motives and intentions are behind such decisions and is not looking to persecute (or prosecute) those who make such choices. We need to look more closely at this subject and bring resolution so we can unite and be at peace with this issue.

It can be a practical decision and should certainly not be relegated to the back alleys, as it was in the terrible times before it became legal. At one time there was so much shame around sexuality and contraception that many lives were ruined; there was little awareness or open discussion. People made choices and, depending on their beliefs, they suffered with them.

From what I understand, the experience of abortion stays in cellular memory. As just mentioned, God knows the circumstances and reasons for the choice, but the woman sometimes cannot forgive herself even if she totally believes she made the right decision. There is some small soul connection between mother and the fetus, particularly when it is further along. The important thing to do in the case of abortion is to create a process for honoring the loss and the change in the path of the soul of the unborn baby. There can still be a spiritual attachment between the mother and the unborn baby even when there is no longer a physical one.

For those who make this choice, it is best to transform the energy so both souls can move on. The woman who has had an abortion could—through an ethical spiritual medium or a qualified regression therapist—have a dialogue with the child's soul. If she feels guilt or regret, she may ask for forgiveness.

This process can initiate a healing process for both the mother and the soul of the unborn child that frees them to go on to their next phase of existence.

*Reincarnation*

From what I have been told by my spirit guides, reincarnation happens. However, not all souls after this life will reincarnate, as this depends on how much evolution is under their belt—they may have completed what they needed to learn in physical form. And there is the issue of whether the soul in this lifetime had the opportunity to complete the tasks and challenges that it may have set up for itself before incarnating. This is of primary importance.

At physical death, the soul will rest between physical lifetimes to the equivalent of two hundred years of our time. However, there are accidents that take place, as when someone dies prematurely or as a young person on the battlefield, that result in the time between lives being much shorter. No doubt these are complex issues and understood better from the spiritual side of the equation.

There is little physical proof surrounding this topic to please the skeptics. Reincarnation is intangible, to say the least. However, there are documented case studies, such as those from Dr. Brian Weiss and many books written on the subject from reputable authors like Edgar Cayce and philosopher, psychologist, and physician Dr. Raymond A. Moody, Jr. who is best known for his best-selling book *Life After Life*.

*Suicide*

When you begin to fully comprehend how the system works—that we as energy beings are born into a physical vessel to experience the gift of physical life—you understand that suicide is pointless. The reality is that one will still come face to face with oneself and others in the heavenly realm—there is no escape. People end up punishing themselves by cutting their life short, inhibiting their ability for progression and many of their soul's reasons for being here. Furthermore, they will likely have to face those same problems in the spiritual realm or return back to a physical life once more. In addition, committing suicide hurts those around them, leaving others in emotional pain with usually more questions than answers.

*Capital Punishment*

Similar to suicide, capital punishment is not a useful answer to resolving the challenges of an individual's life path—the practice of "an eye for an eye" does not address the personal evolution of the person. Each state dictates this level of penalty as it receives a court verdict and enforces the law. It is a *human* law rather than a *spiritual* one that says this individual is a threat to society and cannot be rehabilitated. While obviously there is a financial cost to incarcerating a criminal for life, it is here, looking at oneself inside a jail cell, that some measure of reflection may take place. Otherwise, the execution of a convicted criminal essentially sets the soul free with a limited human experience. It is the earthly existence where great lessons of emotional pain and suffering are encountered, and taking another's life through capital punishment deprives the natural law of cause and effect to flow to the offender. Through execution we end up making a God-like decision and then hope the Creator finds a way to rehabilitate the executed in the afterlife.

## A New Standard

A paradigm shift or new economic model may await us in the future. Military wars, economic conflicts, population growth,

## Principle Three: The Power of Unity

and competition for resources may force us to reevaluate our ways of living if we are to survive and thrive. My hope is that we may reach agreement among ourselves before we are forced to initiate change as a result of revolution or natural disasters, because when transformation is forced upon us it is always harder to accomplish than if we come up with creative alternatives as part of our inherent evolution. With enlightened choices, unity and peace may be possible among all nations.

CHAPTER 7

# PRINCIPLE FOUR:

# SCHOOL IS NEVER OUT

*The difference between school and life?*
*In school you're taught a lesson and given a test.*
*In life, you're given a test that teaches you a lesson.*
—Tom Bodett, brainyquote.com

Learning never stops—the world is a school for the soul. In *Star Trek* terms, this is a "prime directive." Besides expressing love, the acquisition of knowledge and furthering the development of our soul are the reasons why we incarnate.

We learn about ourselves and we learn from others (parents, teachers, friends, adversaries, and so on). We also learn from situations that life deals us. These lessons could include a difficult job decision, a divorce, or an unexpected disappointment that pushes our thinking and emotional construct outside the box of our normal comfort zone.

Knowledge is gained in many places beyond books and academics. Humans are experiential—we learn from *doing*. And, as the saying goes, there is no substitute for actual experience. This is how we expand our emotional and intellectual selves, how we evolve and are then able to pass along these lessons to others. The more this cycle continues, the more we move farther along in our progression. And this process is eternal.

The universe in which we live has many dimensions and realities that comprise a vast flow of energy.[1] When we pass over into the spiritual realm, learning is just as continuous as it was when we were human. We pass our learned lessons on not only to those in the flesh while we are alive, but also to others in spiritual form when we cross over at death. We live as a reference for others to follow. With the discovery of the atom and more recently with quantum physics, modern science is beginning to understand how the smallest particles of energy work and where we may fit in.

Science tells us that energy can be neither created nor destroyed, so where does it go? Or, more specifically, knowing that our true essence consists of energy, where does our life force go when our physical body dies? From what I have witnessed and experienced, this energy is a continuous flow from one reality to another. It is a natural cycle for our physical body to die and our energy/life force to move on to another plane of existence.

I have been blessed to observe the materialization of an intelligent being, in the form of energy, resembling a human form. It does not happen often or for fun, but only with deliberate intention for a purpose of communication. Under the right conditions, beings of light can materialize for the purpose of teaching, guiding, consoling, educating, and helping us move along our path.

These beings can be from the angelic realm, a personal guide, an ascended master (an enlightened spirit), a friend, or a loved one, and they can be from different parts of the nonphysical universe. A friend or a loved one may reside in a lower dimension, while the other beings may come from a higher plane of existence and have different purposes and reasons for their work. Either way, the messages are usually those of love and support for us here on Earth.

*Principle Four: School Is Never Out*

The first time I experienced a "guide" was in Circle as I was attempting to communicate a message to a fellow classmate. I was able to literally feel the energy of another being directly behind me as information was being placed into my thoughts. At first, there was an unusual sensation of heat on the back of my neck. As I became aware of this feeling, the energy began to embrace me in a loving show of support. I felt that this was a validation that the work I was doing in Circle was being acknowledged by those on the other side.

Unlike what you might see in a science fiction movie, there is nothing uncomfortable in experiencing the energy of a nonphysical being firsthand. In a classroom setting, I saw another healer's guide materialize; he had long white hair, and the outline of his figure was an almost translucent grayish-white. It seems that anytime we see something like this we are seeing "light," so it will likely have some of these qualities. The vision will resemble what this individual looked like while he or she was alive in physical form. Other clairvoyants have said to me that spirit energy is capable of materializing to the point where it can be difficult to discriminate the vision from an everyday person. It takes experience to be able to discern what is being shown to us.

People learn in different ways and experience energy differently. Some people are auditory, and some are visual in their learning styles. The same holds true with feelings and kinesthetic senses and how each of us processes information. Depending on your sensory style of picking up information, you may *hear, feel, see,* or *know* that this nonphysical energy is surrounding us.

For example, many people are wired for vision as a primary way of sensory input, so if stimuli come to them in other ways, these impressions do not always register or hold meaning for the person. "Seeing is believing" for a lot of folks, and often we accept only visual perception as proof that something is real. And when people lack this personal visual experience, their acceptance is often not strong enough to carry them through this alternate reality and integrate it into their belief system. I understand this very well, as this is how it initially was for me when I started attending classes in Circle. For a long time I never saw anything, so for many years I was a healthy skeptic while developing. Then, as I persevered with my own awakening, visual experiences began to occur and I became committed to the process.

This other reality, where our deceased loved ones now reside, is not far away in a distant place, but exists all around us at this very moment. Energy, like electricity, is difficult to see with our human eyes, but it can be easier to *feel* and sometimes just to *know* when it is present. This is why some people will say they feel a presence around them or know a deceased loved one is with them.

Unless a person is born "open" with the ability of clairvoyance to see the unseen, the kinesthetic and "feeling" types may have an easier time sensing the energies that are present around us. At this point I find it intriguing when I feel an energy in the air around me, not always knowing precisely what the energy source is or why it has shown up. There can be many reasons for spiritual energy to be present. However, even a nonvisual experience with this energy can lead to belief in this reality rather quickly.

## *Personality versus the Soul*

For most of us our personality or ego, as well as our learned behaviors, usually has some degree of conflict with our spiritual self, our soul. The soul incarnates with one or more objectives to accomplish during its human life that may or may not

## Principle Four: School Is Never Out

take place depending on the whether the ego or personality is making the day-to-day decisions rather than the soul itself. The personality can be led by the soul through life lessons, but there is still no guarantee that the two will be in unison with each other. If there is no conflict, then we are truly living in harmony with the Divine. We usually define ourselves by our physical being, yet it is our soul that is our true self, which lives on long after our flesh and ego self are left behind.

There must be thousands of books written on personality and psychology, yet far fewer about the soul, so most of us are not as familiar with this essential component of ourselves. It is the soul and its journey that are the primary reason for human existence. While all life on this planet has spiritual roots, the intelligence of our soul is what differentiates us from most other life forms on this planet.

The personality is a reflection of all of our experiences since birth and how we react to these events; it can be either a help or a hindrance in allowing the soul to fully experience the human condition. Only the soul knows why it is here, why it has chosen to incarnate at this time, and what lessons and creativity it desires to experience; and these lessons could very well be different from what our personality's desire is to experience. Lessons in the form of experiencing the death of a loved one, a physical or mental disability, illness, or a number of other challenging circumstances may be designed to expand our awareness. Herein lies the potential conflict, as the personality goes on about its rather automatic affairs without regard to the deeper reasons and purposes for life.

There are ways to try to become closer to the soul, such as through meditation, dreaming, expressing creativity, and imagination. Even so, if your soul could pick up a phone from the deep subconscious and tell you why you are here and what lessons you are to learn in this life, you might not believe it.

Your personality or ego will not always wish to experience severe life challenges.

So, there is a process in place whereby each of us has a spirit guide, friend, or what some refer to as a "guardian angel" leading us to situations in life designed for learning. We still have free will to make different choices, yet they are always with us. And, though it may not seem like it in certain circumstances, we are never given more challenges than we can handle.

## Evolution of Knowledge

Everything in life follows a cycle. If you observe the natural world around you, you will see this ring true. The change of seasons, the cycles of plant life, Earth's orbit around the sun, the planet's twenty-four-hour rotation, bird migration, the regular renewing of cells within our bodies, sleep cycles, eating patterns, and even dying are cyclical in nature. Many plants bloom again in the spring after appearing to have "died" during the winter season, and so it is the same with our own human life as it is intertwined with that of Spirit. Our soul, after resting in heaven, may decide it desires to return to a physical form once again for more experience and understanding.

We are here for learning, acquiring knowledge, and to give and receive love. At the death of our physical body, we take all of this experience with us into the spiritual dimension and the Universal Mind that connects all of us. This knowledge helps others in spirit form as well as those who remain in the physical dimension. The life cycle and partnership between those here and those in the spiritual realm is never ending. It is subtle and continuous, and it furthers evolution on both sides.

Through reincarnation there is a constant cycling of learning over and over again between worlds. In my communication with spirit entities, it is indicated that reincarnation affects each soul and each person in its own way. Each soul is unique in its purpose; therefore its life path, too, has its own course.

## Swimming with the Current

A valuable blueprint for making life run smoothly is to embrace difficult situations as opportunities for learning and personal growth. We need to move away from questioning, *Why me?* On some level we find ourselves in circumstances by choice or as the product of our past decisions that have a type of domino effect. It does not mean we are being punished. It is as if we are maneuvering around our own misdirections that often have unforeseen consequences. Surprisingly, there are times when we are led to these difficulties by a higher power, our soul self. Some people refer to this as the "higher self," and it is the part of us that is connected through the subconscious mind to the Universal Mind connecting us all.

Our higher self has an expanded vision of why we may be at a potential crossroad in our life and the purpose underlying the trials that we are experiencing. The higher self is looking at the big picture, seeking spiritual growth, and is not as concerned about moment-to-moment occurrences.

In our physical beings, our perceptions may be clouded. We may not understand the natural flow of our lives and as a result may fight against it as we disagree with what we experience. How we respond is a huge test of faith in a Higher Power that knows and understands what path is best for us to follow.

↭ *The life we have is a gift; the harsh experiences we endure are lessons that move us forward and build inner strength. When we eventually look back, only then will we see our experiences with clarity, when their meanings were initially shrouded for us. Try understanding this now so you may rise up to your current challenges and not fear what life throws your way.* ↭

When Spirit begins leading us in a direction, we take on the lead role of our own screenplay. Sometimes, events and coincidences are brought in to support the unique path our life is taking. Through free will, we always have choices for making decisions that move us forward in personal growth or keep us where we are. According to spiritual teacher and the author of *Journey into Now*, Leonard Jacobson, "Everything that occurs in your life is an opportunity for awakening."[2]

Many of these choices can be challenging to make; that is the test. They may even require soul searching and sacrifice; their purpose may not always be immediately clear. There are many reasons why a circumstance presents itself, as the life lessons we each face are different depending on where we are on our own path. You may have to hold your breath and just keep moving through the difficult times. However, if the decision feels in alignment with your inner core, you will know that you are working with the divine plan. If we make decisions that resonate with the path that our higher self is mapping out for us, we usually feel lighter and more at peace with our decisions.

In a difficult circumstance, more than likely we will be challenged to act with our heart as well as our head. This is a common lesson for us in physical reality, especially in a society that is fast moving and impersonal, keeping our minds continually engaged. It is in our hearts where real personal growth takes place, and as it is usually an underused muscle, it often seeks to protect itself from internal or external emotional threats. When this type of lesson confronts us, the decisions will not be easy and emotions will surface. Let them! We need to remember that this is exactly the learning process necessary for our soul's growth.

When there are great challenges and heavy burdens to carry, we sometimes wonder, *Why is this happening to me?* or

## Principle Four: School Is Never Out

*Why does this always happen to me?* The answer is that lessons, through obstacles placed in our path, continue occurring until we learn, embrace the change, and expand within the lesson. Sometimes we have to learn how to lose before we can learn how to win.

After I left the big firms on Wall Street to work on my own, I thought that given my experience it would be easy. This was far from the truth. I stumbled many times, needing to learn lessons in empathy and understanding before I could build a practice that served individuals. Indeed, there were a number of years of challenging learning situations before I succeeded.

If you look at professional sports, you will observe that there are teams that come so close to winning but ultimately end up in defeat. Then, the following year, as a result of the lesson of failure, they put it all together and take the championship. Even in political races we see a candidate run for office and come up short, only to learn from his or her mistakes and achieve victory the next time around. Kuan Yin, the East Asian bodhisattva of compassion, expresses it this way: "Through sorrow we learn joy, through poverty we learn to appreciate riches, and through laughter you better understand the salt of tears. Are these not true lessons in life?"[3]

No matter what is occurring for you, try to understand that we are never alone, especially when faced with difficult issues in our lives. Besides our friends, family members, and confidants with whom we surround ourselves, we are also surrounded by loving beings on the other side of the veil—from heaven. They are always there to support us, and it is as important to them as it is to us that we continue learning and fulfilling the chosen purpose for our soul. The ascended master White Eagle expresses it this way: "Love on the other side is waiting to catch us."[4] Knowing this to be the case, we can experience life's hardships, understanding there is a support structure in place that knows about our struggles as we move through our earthly lessons.

There is a perpetual cosmic dance that plays over and over like a beautiful ballet. What we may perceive as random events placing us in the middle of chaos can be viewed with much precision and satisfaction by those in the nonphysical realm. They know that the bigger the challenge is for us, the greater is the lesson. And the saying "God does not give us anything we cannot handle" rings true.

Eventually, with the passing of time, hopefully we will look back even with laughter and confidence that we persevered through the tough circumstances. When this happens, then we are ready for our next lesson. Even better, with our experience and knowledge we are in a position to help others. And so the cycle continues.

## *Hopelessness Is an Illusion*

When in the throes of despair it is difficult, if not impossible, to perceive that there is a soul lesson unfolding. From this perspective, one cannot make sense of the sudden death of a young mother, an unforeseen severe disability, the starvation of a family, a terminal illness, or the loss of an innocent child. However, the pain that we experience when left behind after tragedy can transform our understanding and appreciation in a way that may not have been achieved by any other method. There is an irony and a truth wrapped together as one.

Sometimes, we may feel that everything is working against us for no apparent reason. Our situation may resemble chaos, which can be the result of our own decisions creating disruptions in our normal flow of being. Once our energy finds its right place, a calmness takes hold, and the perception that things were out of balance disappears. Chaos is the universe

## Principle Four: School Is Never Out

seeking realignment—often from the disharmony we as humans have created.

With regard to alignment, we may control our own energy, but we cannot control anyone else's. A common mistake people make when seeking control in their lives is to try to control others around them. Even if the personality of the one being controlled is subservient, at some point the person's internal compass will point in another direction, and conflict will ensue between the two parties. Given enough time, this type of relationship backfires, as the energy of being controlled and contained seeks to find a balance in freedom.

Surprisingly, there are situations where a child is born with the *intention* of an early death. While this may be hard for us to grasp and seems implausible, from a spiritual perspective some situations can be set in advance for teaching wisdom. Perhaps, in this case, the family experiences a depth of love and compassion that may not have occurred otherwise than through the loss of this child. The child (soul), once in heaven, now comprehends the full picture; it understands its earthly role quite well and does not see this as painful. The child's soul may also learn from this experience just from observing the emotions and actions of the parents. Herein is the perfection of planning and focus by the unseen forces that operate within the fabric of our lives.

It is important to acknowledge that our interaction with these unseen forces is a collaboration: as we grow, those in spirit grow too. What we do affects them, and what they do affects us. One is not mutually exclusive of the other. We are all together in this adventure called life!

However, as we have "free will" for making decisions from moment-to-moment, much in how our lives unfold is not preordained. We can and often do affect the results with our sudden decisions. There is always probability and outcome.

We will likely act and behave a certain way given a set of circumstances, but there is no guarantee. In addition, there can be a random act or decision that changes everything.

For example, if we own a retail store, perhaps an opportunity for us is being orchestrated by those in the spiritual realm with someone walking by our store. This person receives inspiration as he or she looks in our storefront window; it motivates him or her to walk in. It turns out that this person "happens" to be in a related business for the goods we sell and begins talking to us about an opportunity for our business. There is no guarantee that the person walking in the store will offer us the opportunity to do business with him or her. Neither is there a guarantee that we, after hearing the offer, will be interested in accepting the terms of the proposal. It comes down to the probability of the situation and the free will all parties have to accept the connection Spirit has put in motion. Again, probability and outcome are at work, and it is all done with the highest integrity and love that Spirit has for seeing us succeed.

Here is another example: You have a random thought about someone you haven't seen for months, and later in the day you happen to bump into her. One explanation is that you may be picking up the thoughts of this other person psychically, as we are all psychic to some extent. However, it is also possible that a higher source is prearranging this "chance" meeting, and so this energy is in the air. There are reasons these seeming chance meetings occur beyond what we are capable of understanding. One possibility might be that there is some unfinished business between parties even if we do not understand it.

*In reality, there are very few chance coincidences, as there are reasons for everything. However, we can only perceive things from our limited point of view. As we are usually wrapped up in our own thoughts, this also clouds our perception as to the larger reality surrounding us all.*

## Principle Four: School Is Never Out

When I was young, I had a breakup with a longtime girlfriend while away from school on a semester break from college. She used the vacation period intentionally to break things off, as she knew it would be next to impossible to do this if we were physically together. However, I knew that if I could speak with her in person I might fix things, and it was my strong intention to do so.

In planning my return to school, there were numerous ways I could have traveled—car, bus, or plane—as well as quite a number of days and times to pick. And, as far as I was aware, I had randomly picked a day to return by plane. Yet, upon my return to school, a strange thing happened that even to this day I find difficult to believe. While I was sitting inside the plane as people were boarding, my ex-girlfriend walked over and sat in the seat next to me! The odds of this occurring were astronomical, and, yes, we were back together for another two years. There seemed to be unfinished business on one level or another. We do not always consciously know what lessons our souls seek for their own understanding.

### Personal Lessons

Continuing on the topic of lessons, life challenges in the areas of confidence and self-esteem can be opportunities to strengthen your inner core. If these are the areas of growth that are up for you, you may find yourself in situations where you need to be self-reliant. Perhaps your boss selected you of all the people in your department to make an important speech, yet you are frightened of public speaking. Once this task is completed, however, having overcome your insecurity and risen to the challenge can be very satisfying.

Issues of trust with others often indicate personal matters of being hurt. If you have these concerns, you may find yourself in a position where you need to trust or be trusted. If you fail, you may find yourself experiencing trust issues over and over until you finally learn the lesson.

Matters of the heart can be even more complex. The more you protect yourself, the less open your heart will be, which is the opposite of why you are in this physical reality in the first place. A very simple example is around deep personal relationships. One cannot expect to share a life with another human being if one is afraid of the vulnerability that being in love brings. I learned this firsthand. Ten years before I was married I was engaged to another woman. When this broke off, I closed my heart to avoid being hurt again. Even though I met several great women, I allowed these opportunities to slip away rather than trusting the process. Eventually, I realized that the only one who lost out during that time was me.

Not all personal lessons are emotional issues; some take physical form. Your body is more than just alive—it has intelligence. This intelligence knows to attack an intruder when germs are present. It knows to transmit pain signals when you are hurt. It regulates many complex systems that are integrated throughout the body. We take for granted that this happens automatically. Some bodies do not work as well as others, so it is truly a blessing if you have good health. However, as was the case for me, occasionally a person has something important to learn when experiencing ill health.

Your body has the intelligence to teach lessons. If we refer back to the earlier chapter on emotions, we already know that certain types of illness can be traced back to particular emotional issues. The body, in concert with a higher influence, stands ready to transmit disease or pain as a form of communication that things are not well internally. And, as happened to me, if your higher self or a higher power really wants your attention, then you could get dealt a serious illness, redirecting you in life.

*Principle Four: School Is Never Out*

Herein lies the power struggle throughout life between your personality (ego) and your higher self (soul)—your ego may fear change and want the comfort of things remaining the same, while your soul wants you to grow and expand beyond all your self-imposed limitations. Life is an awakening; as lessons come your way you begin seeing things that you may not have been ready or able to see when they first appeared. Or sometimes you do see what is right in front of you, but you do not have the courage or clarity to make the changes that are beneficial. Also, people tend to absorb lessons and information at different rates. A shift in ourself is not a function of intellect, but rather a function of readiness and a willingness to see things from a different perspective. It is at this point that we change.

## The Earth as a Teacher

We have examined the nature of our reality, the ways we can take charge of our emotions, and how we can change our thinking about our life lessons. We all have individual choices, and we also have choices as a society. If we learn who we are and how much spiritual power we possess by harnessing love and hope and overcoming fear, the outcome of our mutual futures can be the way the Creator intended.

We are currently being cautioned by those in heaven about possible outcomes for our planet. There are changes and energy shifts that we can acknowledge and use to shift the destructive course we are on, or we can continue to receive some very difficult lessons. What we do now will have far-reaching consequences—long after we join our loved ones in the spiritual dimension. But the expression "As above, so below" means that our choices here in the material realm also have an impact upon those nonphysical beings whose souls wish to move on to higher levels of being. We may hold back their progression, as well as the movement of the future, by what we do in the here and now. There are changes coming to this world; some have already begun, and we are going to need to prepare for more.

There were many dire predictions about 2012 from the Mayan prophecies, the Hopi Indians, Nostradamus, and a few others calling for great changes that could lead to death and destruction. However, the world obviously did not come to an end in December 2012, and many people are left with bulk items they hoarded in their storage bunkers. Nevertheless, the spiritual "shift" spoken of is indeed in the process of taking place, and the years ahead will bring many changes to the paths of countless people.

Our Creator, Source, God, Allah, Tunkashila, Lord, Great Spirit—whatever your terminology is for the higher power responsible for the universe—believes in the human race. This Creator believes in the potential of our species and loves humankind, as well as all manifested life forms. However, as its children we too are taught lessons, just as parents teach lessons to their children.

When parents send their children to their rooms as punishment, this does not mean that they do not love them. In fact, they likely love their children very much and want them to learn right from wrong. This consequence is a form of *discipline*, a word derived from the word *disciple*, which means "one who accepts the doctrines of another and assists in spreading or implementing them."

Children are disciples of their parents, who hope to teach them the right way to live in the world based on their own wisdom. The parents hope that their children grow up to be even better than they are and that the kids can eventually take their place as adults who continue the good work. So it is similar with our Creator and us as its children. We are now in line for learning a great lesson of compassion. It is time to stop

## Principle Four: School Is Never Out

thinking, *What can I take from my neighbor?* and start asking, *What does he or she need?*

The planet we live on is alive—Earth has a consciousness that is her own too. Just like plant life, she is affected by what we do physically to her, as well as by the positive and negative emotional and mental energies we direct toward her. And just as we do, our planet, which is also a life form, has the ability to take direction from a Higher Power. And she may be doing so, as evidenced in part in the many weather-pattern changes we have been seeing in recent years.

There is and has been an ongoing debate as to the validity of global climate change. There are well-respected scientists and researchers on both sides of this argument. The global-warming discussion primarily centers on the temperature changes in the air, and since the air temperatures have not changed much this debate rages on. Perhaps there should be more conversation on water temperatures because this is where the energy changes are coming from.

One does not need to be a scientist to see that the polar bears are running out of places to live. Neither does one need to be a researcher to remember that a tsunami killed nearly 250,000 people one weekend in Indonesia a few years ago. More recently, Japan nearly had a nuclear meltdown from an earthquake and a tsunami.

Below the Pacific Ocean lies the "Ring of Fire," where 452 volcanoes, or 75 percent of the world's active and dormant volcanoes, are located.[5] The Ring of Fire consists of several tectonic plates in Earth's crust that extend from Southeast Asia all the way north to Alaska, then west to California and south along the coast of South America. Ninety percent of the world's earthquakes occur in this region of the world.[6] This energy and releasing of the heat are throwing the planet into a new paradigm. Earth's inner core is spinning faster and heating up layers beneath the plates that rest upon this surface. This creates friction, which results in heat that is finding its way aboveground to our atmosphere.[7]

From 1995 through 2011, this energy release in the Pacific was responsible for a number of huge tragedies, with earthquakes and tsunamis causing hundreds of thousands of deaths and trillions in economic destruction. And the frequency and magnitude are increasing over time. These effects may be the indicator of a domino effect around the world, where energy released from below is causing imbalances in land and water pressure or the melting of ice at the poles.

Dr. Tony Phillips of *Science News* (NASA news), has indicated that about 400 polar shifts have occurred during the past 330 million years, with an average interval of 200,000 years.[8] And, according to *The Independent*, the North Pole is moving toward Russia at the rate of 40 miles per day, which is 33 percent faster than prior to 1989.[9] I am not a scientist, but I can see that this information translates into disruptions and displacement of land and water. Truthfully, I would like to hope that this information is incorrect, but hard as it is to believe, such catastrophes may have happened before in Earth's history. So, this may not be so far-fetched.

Some of the changes have already begun and will occur more rapidly in the years ahead. The systems we have in place now are adequate in the developed world, but fragile. Many people in other areas of the globe may receive the food and energy they need for sustenance, yet it takes very little to interfere with their basic needs. Even now, when disruption occurs people lose their energy, heat, and hot water easily, and for longer and longer periods of time.

The population continues growing as if Earth has an infinite supply of raw materials whenever we want them. We know this is not true, yet we act in a brazen manner as if we are entitled to these things. A wake-up call may be in the not-too-distant future. Future generations of people are depending on us now to act responsibly to head off the tragedy of planetary disaster.

In the meantime, we need to take inventory of ourselves and our families. We need to think about what we are doing and how we can help each other. When there was a 2014 storm warning that threatened to shut down electricity in New York, people hoarded batteries and flashlights. Perhaps we can examine this reactive behavior of "us against them" mentality. Our reaction rather could be about how we will help each other in the event of a weather emergency. Can we make sure everyone has batteries and water? We shouldn't have to rely on disaster relief and its limited resources if we take others into account when preparing for the unexpected.

What is being communicated by the Divine is that there will be geological changes made to the Earth in the future—not a cataclysm, but maybe great displacements in land and water, throwing us into a state of flux. This energy release might be on a massive scale. As a civilization we will need to show "compassion" for one another and to rely to support each other as we go through any period of change.

Please be aware that the message I received relative to the preceding information was put forth in a loving and supportive way. This communication was clear, and so was the fact that once this disruptive period passes, a very bright future for humankind is ahead—there will be a new beginning for all of us.

PART THREE

# Embracing Your Soul's Journey

*What you state, you create.*
—Wallace Wattles, goodreads.com

CHAPTER 8

# PRINCIPLE FIVE:

# Creating Is Always in Season

*Know that it is not all just to live—not all just to be good, but good for something; that ye may fulfill that purpose for which ye have entered this experience.*

—Edgar Cayce, goodreads.com

Throughout the ages, humanity has sought expression through different means. In art we see this illustrated as far back as history dates. We see it on cave walls, the ceiling of the Sistine Chapel at the Vatican, and as a breathtaking display in the form of pyramids in Egypt.

Personal expression through creativity is more than painting and drawing. It shows up in music, writing, poetry, photography, film making, clothing styles, food preparation, home decor, automobiles, landscaping, websites, tattoos, and just about everything our eyes see or our ears hear.

And, although many of us take it for granted, this same personal expression by great thinkers has fostered creativity in inventions and technology. Notable inventors such as Thomas Edison, Archimedes, Ben Franklin, Nikola Tesla, Alexander Graham Bell, the Wright Brothers, Leonardo da Vinci, Galileo,

Marie Curie, Henry Ford, and Steve Jobs have all managed to use their creativity to move the human race farther along on its evolutionary path.

When we look at the body of the industrial and technological revolutions in the past 2½ centuries, it is awe inspiring that so much progress has been accomplished in such a short period of humankind's history. It does not seem by chance that the expansion of freedom in personal expression after the 1960s social revolution in the United States led to a massive expression in creativity through technology—resulting in a technological revolution throughout the world. This says a great deal about our potential as a race of beings, as well as the creativity buried deep within all of us just waiting to come forth into form.

When speaking of God and how the human race came about, people often refer to "his or its creation" (depending on their religious tradition). Therefore, in a subtle, yet significant, way we are seeing Spirit expressing itself through us and using creativity with who we are. If we are made in the image of our Source, then creating is a natural ability we all possess and need to foster.

The ability for each of us to be creatively expressive is unique, and so the differences among us should be embraced rather than judged. Education may result in a more refined expression, but the core essence in each of us is there before education takes hold. ᭥ *Race, religion, education, age, sex, financial resources, looks, and size have no correlation with the great well of expression that resides within us.* ᭥

It is never too late to begin or to continue creating. This is a reason why we are here, and sometimes it takes an emotional jolt—such as the loss of a job, the death of a loved one, or a divorce—to get us to wake up to the realization that we have not yet fully expressed the life we were meant to live. This is

## Principle Five: Creating Is Always in Season

not to assume that we are unhappy. The thunderbolt throws us off balance, and when we regain our footing our perspective may change. We see that all along we may have been unaware of what life is presenting to us. When these events take place, we may be forced into an awakening. We start asking more powerful questions of ourselves and looking for answers. And questions build bridges to new places and fresh experiences.

My life is a perfect example of this. When I faced my own mortality, I changed my perspective and saw things differently. I asked many "why" questions of myself, my relationships, and my Maker. At first, it was confusing. Then I began to see life with more clarity as my awareness became heightened. As I worked with the Circle, I realized that this new insight was all it took for my perspective of life to shift to one where I asked what I could do for others instead of what they might do for me.

It is never too late to understand the power each of us has for creating our own realities, changing our lives, or living differently. It is our mind, through learned behaviors, that structures how we live. There is a power—the soul—in our heart and in our gut that speaks to us, that fuels the creativity to break these preconceived structures. Once you choose to open yourself to your soul and to what is within you, there is no going back. This is the natural progression for our evolution.

In time, we become more in tune with our heart and our inner voice—often also referred to as our intuition, our soul, the voice of God in us, or our gut feelings—rather than having our mind dominate. Too often our mind tells us one thing, while our heart and intuition are pulling us elsewhere. One is not necessarily better than the others; however, over time, if you notice many conflicts between your heart, gut feelings, and mind, this is an indication you are out of alignment with yourself—your personality and your soul may be in conflict. If this is the case, it is time for a self-assessment as to why this is so. Usually, the more authentic part of yourself will reside in your heart and your intuition.

In this process, there are no judgments—no "right" or "wrong" decisions—to urgently make. Just know that you have the right to change your life and reflect what your heart and your inner voice may be telling you. It might be less stressful if you reach this conclusion by listening early on without the necessity of a life-changing event showing up to get your attention. But either way—creating a motivating force or more intentionally bringing alignment between your heart, your gut feelings, and your mind—will bring your own being into harmony.

Think of your life as a clean canvas that you paint and create as you see fit. Some people know that life is a gift, yet many do not. They get caught up in the bumps in the road instead of continuing to move forward. It is not hard to look around and see those who have still to discover the opportunities with which they have been presented. Life moves quickly, so you need to have gratitude for what you have, keep a clear mind, and seize the day.

☙ *It is important to emphasize that everything you do in this life counts for something. Everything you say in the spoken word affects others. Everything you think affects you. You matter.* ☙ Never underestimate your value or your importance to the overall balance and harmony in the universe. We are all interconnected in the chain of life, and when one link breaks it affects the chain.

All is known and observed by those in heaven, and there are no judgments to be made about us by them, only life lessons to be brought to our awareness and to learn. You have the freedom to choose, so it is up to you. And sometimes the choice isn't between something that is "right" and something that is "wrong"—occasionally things *are just the way they are supposed to be* and we need to accept them. For example, if you grew up wanting to be an artist and your parents wished you to be a doctor, you are not wrong for following your instincts; you listened to your inner voice, and your life is as it is supposed to be. Or, if you followed your heart and ended up marrying a man or a woman outside your faith, then you are being authentic. Judgment is not necessary—leave it for a Higher Power that better understands the dynamics of who we are and the journey each of us is on. I have learned that if we follow our heart, it will likely lead us to our aspirations being fulfilled. And, if not, then there will be fulfillment on some level or another if we are in alignment with our heart.

## *Embrace Your Truth*

In your evolutionary growth, strive to be the best you can be. "Aim high," as my late aunt once said. Have goals to pursue, and try to improve yourself while helping others around you. The poet and philosopher Ralph Waldo Emerson advised, "The creation of a thousand forests is in one acorn. Make yourself necessary to somebody."[1] And, I would add, always be true to yourself in the process.

Once, in the company of a talented spiritual medium, I asked questions about a personal situation that was bothering me. She was presenting me with information when a higher being stepped in to give the medium additional wisdom to share. As it was a difficult time for me, I asked about acting one way or another to remedy the situation, and the response was very simple: "Be who you are."

If you push forward and become someone you are not, you permit yourself to fall back into the same state you were in before. Be genuine, and remember that you are here for a purpose that is equally as important as anyone else's in this world.

As Shakespeare said, "To thine own self be true." ❧ *Birds do not become butterflies; there is a natural order to the universe. You must always be true to yourself; otherwise, your emotions will fester. Evolution will always occur in its own rhythm and time—for you and those whose lives you touch.* ❧

The British novelist J. K. Rowling became famous for writing the "Harry Potter" series of books, yet her life had not always been glamorous and successful. In fact, her situation before writing that overwhelmingly popular series was rather emotionally charged and financially burdened. She had a marriage that ended in divorce and such money problems that she lived out of her car for a while.

It was not until Rowling was inspired to write her first Harry Potter book, and maintained her focus in the midst of harsh difficulties, that things began to come together for her. Even after writing it, a number of publishers rejected her before she finally found one who would take her. Once she found the courage to move forward and the persistence to stay with it, there was no stopping her. Now, J. K. Rowling is estimated to be one of Britain's wealthiest women.[2] States basketball Hall of Famer Michael Jordan, "I have failed over and over again in my life. And that's precisely why I succeed."[3]

## Loving What You Do

What a difference it makes when you are passionate about what you are doing! When you are fully engaged and love what you do, it increases your focus, raises your energy level, and makes a huge impact in your performance. To put it simply, more passion equals performance enhancement. The reason is twofold: (1) Your focus is razor sharp, as the mind fully embraces the task at hand; and (2) the creative energy from the lower chakras flows through you, acting as a battery for

## Principle Five: Creating Is Always in Season

the rest of your being. Your passion continues fueling all your energy centers, and you are ready to take on the world.

This is the link between mind and body: healthy mind, healthy body. When the mind is happy, secure, and without stress, the energy flows through these "open" energy centers. When we are passionate and our emotional state is healthy, our energy centers will work as they are supposed to. Following your path in life and living a life with passion helps open your energy centers so they work to their full capacity. Your body responds, and harmony follows.

"Think on this," said Edgar Cayce in "Reading 4047-2": "The purpose in life, then, is not the gratifying of the appetites nor of any selfish desires, but it is that the entity, the soul, may make the Earth, where the entity finds its consciousness, a better place in which to live."[4]

### The Power of Intention

In time, you will evolve with whatever direction you set your mind to. This is called the "power of intention." It is a universal law that illustrates how powerful you are in creating your own destiny through your thoughts and choices. Focus your mind with intention, and your ability to accomplish goals will increase tenfold. This is the way your mind interacts with life, whether you are consciously aware of it or not.

There are teachers and self-empowerment coaches who speak of this power of intention, which brings about the manifestation of your desired results. Intention brings discipline and focus to the mind. The power of intent raises the vibration of your thoughts so that divine influences can assist you with your goal. The burden is still on *you*, but you may get some help from the other side if your desires are ethical—such as service or help for others—and not for selfish desires. Most people do not understand the connection, or bridge, that is built through thought to the world beyond our senses.

There are those in heaven who are happy to open doors for us. Our friends there take their role in our evolution very seriously. The relationship is reciprocal, as we all progress together as one. *Try being open to this truth and see this for yourself what happens when you put your mind to something with intention. Trust your feelings and have faith that you are well supported by a higher power.*

Here is a four-step process for the power of intention:

1. Know your purpose—what you want to accomplish.
2. You must remove all doubt—really believe it.
3. Expect the desired results—ahead of time.
4. Don't get in your own way—go with the current and flow of life.

Anything you do with your imagination is a form of creative expression. Even problem solving offers the opportunity for creativity. Using intention with a deliberate focus of your mind on what you desire to accomplish is one of the secrets to success in life. The forces on the other side of the veil do not waste energy—they operate with discipline. The more certain you are about what you desire, the easier it is for spirit beings to assist you.

The ideas you generate through your mind rise up from your subconscious or soul to your conscious self. Dr. Carl Jung believed that we all connect from our everyday conscious self to a subconscious or soul deep within us. Our subconscious is then connected to an all-encompassing Universal Mind in which all are linked.[5]

Think of it this way: When you are on your computer using files, this is similar to your everyday conscious self. When you need to search for files and stored information, you search

## Principle Five: Creating Is Always in Season

within your hard drive, which is similar to your subconscious self. Eventually, you may need to look further, so you move from your computer's hard drive outward to the Internet, where you are infinitely connected with everyone and everything. This is an analogy as to how the Universal Mind functions.

Right now, our mind has this power to access information and problem-solve through meditation. When we can step aside and surrender our conscious thoughts, we may enter a deeper, quieter state to receive inspiration. In this deeper state, our conscious mind quiets and our subconscious mind draws near. It is in this state that we may give ourself the power of suggestion or listen quietly for an answer to a question or problem. When we are in deep meditation or asleep, we are in a state of being able to connect with our subconscious and/or the Universal Mind. It is here that a great wealth of creativity awaits you. Setting the intention for problem solving and imagination, which is the language Spirit uses to inspire us, before going to bed makes a huge difference. Your mind is capable of many things, so it helps to establish a direction before retiring. Practice using the power of intention combined with disciplined focus and patience, and you will surely see results over time.

The words and information contained in this book are more than conscious, random thoughts. Some of this material is and was already in my conscious and subconscious minds; there were experiences that needed telling. However, there was also information contained in my subconscious and downloaded to me during the night from the Universal Mind, while in the dream state. Each morning upon awakening, my mind was full of information that I felt urgently needed to be written down. And much of this wisdom is shared with you here.

Many artists in film and music will say that when awaking from sleep, there are new thoughts and ideas on what they need for creating. When your conscious, waking mind moves aside during sleep, a well of vast information is readily accessible. Some of this will be remembered in the morning and some will not; instead, it may trickle into your everyday self over time. Beatle Paul McCartney once stated in an interview that he received ideas for his music in a similar fashion.[6]

What is important is that we use our freedom for creative expression for helping one another—not just for competition that enables us to get ahead. Says author Betty Eddie, "Whatever we become here in mortality is meaningless unless it is done for the benefit of others. Our gifts and talents are given to us to help us serve. And, in serving others, we grow spiritually."[7] We all have the ability to access divine ideas, information, and creative expression. Connecting to the Universal Mind is embracing who you already are; you do it during sleep all the time.

## Life Is a Cocreation

Nature is all around us, and it is constantly creating by expansion and contraction—above you in the sky, below you in the ground, out in the seas, at the highest mountaintop, and even in the air you breathe. Still, many people mistakenly believe that the world revolves around them. I am not referring here to their individual egos so much as to the ego of the collective, the human race.

Much of humanity tends to believe they are above all else, and they justify this by the obvious ability they have for verbal communication. However, intelligence comes in many forms; scientists and animal researchers know this is true. An aggressive virus has intelligent instincts, as does plant life on this planet. Yet too many continually go about their business from day to day as if they inhabit Earth all alone and that it exists solely to serve *them*.

*Principle Five: Creating Is Always in Season*

We, as people, are an important piece of the puzzle on our beloved planet. Interaction with our environment is necessary, but *dominating* it with reckless intent will come back to haunt us. We interconnect with everything around us, but we are not more essential than any other living thing here. Pollution, overfishing, toxic waste, and diminished natural resources are just a few examples of how our actions have disrespected life around us. What are the early consequences of this behavior? Rising cancer rates, famine, species elimination, lung diseases, and a fight for survival are just a few.

Our ability for creating and expanding civilization depends greatly on our ability to coexist with all the life forms on our planet. Ignoring this simple truth places us in direct conflict with nature. And, as we have seen throughout history, we are no match for Mother Nature.

Coming from the business world, I understand the role large corporations have in providing global services as well as maximizing their bottom line. Conflicts arise in generating profits for the company versus what may be right for civilization and our beloved Earth. Can we not figure out a way to reward the corporation that does good for this world at its own expense? Let us collaborate with this great planet we live on to serve all her inhabitants.

CHAPTER 9

## PRINCIPLE SIX:

# The Orchestra behind the Scenes

*The love that we offer must come in different . . . ways because the nurturing and the nourishment has to be tuned to the capacity of the recipient.*

—Archangel Ariel, in Interview with an Angel, by Stevan J. Thayer and Linda Sue Nathanson

No person is alone in eternity unless it is his or her vision from the Creator to be so. We can trust that we are always looked after by those in heaven, the spiritual dimension of existence. There is beautifully orchestrated "music" playing in the background while we are going about our daily lives. The music is God's, that of our ancestors, and those in spirit form who have an interest in our success while we are in physical form.

Yes, we have all probably wondered at one time, *Is anyone out there watching over me?* As was demonstrated in the inspirational 1946 James Stewart movie *It's a Wonderful Life*, with the guardian angel Clarence offering assistance to the totally demoralized George Bailey, this relationship does exist. Both my personal experience and my guides from the other side have said that we all have at least one in spirit form that is with us from birth until the day we die, and this guide has dedicated itself "in service" for watching over us for our entire life.

In some cases, we have more than one spirit friend who accompanies us on this human journey. Depending on what vocation we choose or the direction for our lives, we may have a specific guide that comes to assist for a particular time period and situation and then moves on to help another person. And when loved ones pass over, they too may stay around us for a while.

You may call them angels, guides, spirit friends, guardians, or whatever your belief system tells you. The bottom line is that they are here and remain for our benefit, as well as for a learning experience for themselves. You may ask, how do they learn? As a former teacher, I can say I learned more from the material when teaching it than I ever did learning it as a student.

It took me years to finally believe they were real, even though there were many validations along the way. My upbringing and left-brain wiring put up defenses for accepting this as true. However, I became so sensitive to the finer energies around me that I could not help but *feel* and eventually *see* their presence. I finally realized, much to my amazement, that they had been there all along.

It does not matter whether you believe this as your truth or whether you desire this or not—it happens anyway. Most of these beings were once incarnated just as you and I, and they understand the difficulties and challenges we undertake each day. Others are a higher order in spirit form from the beginning of creation and never walked upon Earth. Regardless, they are all here to help.

✽ *Know that in their eyes, success is not defined by money or power but rather by our happiness, our peace, and whether we are able to fulfill our purpose for incarnating.* ✽ I can't express enough or too often that experiencing the human condition

*Principle Six: The Orchestra behind the Scenes*

is an important gift not to be wasted and that help is available for us to accomplish the purpose that brought us here. But too many of us take our lives for granted, not understanding the significant interconnections each of us has within the whole.

Most of our spirit guides had their human existence at one time, plus they have had learning while in spirit form, which makes them perfectly suitable for guiding us. Their satisfaction comes from knowing they are helping us on our path. And the relationship is symbiotic: as we learn, they learn, and vice versa.

It is their love, patience, and understanding for *who we are* rather than any directives they give us that help us in our lives. Ultimately, we always have free will for making our own decisions and personal choices; nobody tells us what to do, particularly our guides. They do not interfere in our daily lives. They are not here to make choices for us. Rather, they are here to *support* us. This is our Earth walk, for better or for worse. Just as in school, we cannot learn if someone else does the work for us.

## Angels among Us

After several years of development in Circle and raising my vibration, my energy centers were wide open, and I began experiencing communication with spiritual influences. This occurred through hearing, feeling, and sometimes even sight. It was not an easy process, as I naturally resisted and questioned, but once I allowed it to happen the floodgates opened. My psychic senses expanded, raising my awareness to the energies around us.

Those in heaven are always waiting for those who are willing and able to cross the bridge halfway from our existence to theirs. It is on this bridge that they will meet and begin to guide us, if we allow ourselves to be open to it. To be more specific, I am referring here to angels and guides and occasionally even loved ones who have passed over. The assistance given is always loved based and working for our benefit—nothing more complicated. The guidance only becomes difficult when we allow doubt and fear to override our heart.

Once we have experienced this communication and partnership with the universe, we start taking inventory of our own selves and assessing what is important in life. We begin seeing our world differently, understanding how special we all are and the need for us to not waste the time we have together. We then recognize the power of unity both here in the physical and also with those who are in the spiritual dimension.

So, how do you get to know your spirit guide? Well, even for me this still remains a learning process. You do not just arrive home from work and see your guide watching the TV or eating donuts with coffee. Your guide or guides are with you all the time, sometimes very close and occasionally viewing your situation from a distance. Always, though, they are just a thought away from you. Your guides become attuned to your frequency of thoughts and know when they are needed.

With regular meditation and leading an ethical life, you may quiet the mind with intention and raise your energy vibration by attuning your thoughts to those in heaven. This will help bring you closer to where these spiritual beings reside. From this point, you may ask for a sign to know you are not alone. Seeing them is not common, so you are more likely to *hear* or *feel* those in spirit around you. You may feel heat on the back of your neck, feel goose bumps on your skin, or even hear a whisper in your ear. These are the more common ways that they let us know they are there.

You can ask for help by focusing your thoughts as you might in prayer. And no, this is not three wishes from a genie in a bottle! As "help" may come about in many forms and may not be readily identifiable, you may believe initially that no one

## Principle Six: The Orchestra behind the Scenes

heard your prayer. You must understand that receiving direct help could offset the lesson and life challenge that have crossed your path. This does not mean assistance is not forthcoming. You may be receiving inspiration in the form of ideas or nuggets of creativeness in your mind, although you may not recognize this as a form of help or support. Receiving more concrete help than flashes of insight may negate the expansion of life experience that potentially occurs from your challenges. Thus, assistance in the form of inspiration can be intentional. Often, with good intentions those beings conspire to inspire.

Those beyond the veil know our true selves and the talents we have better than we do. ❧ *The truth is that we all have gifts, even though some of us never open them up.* ❧ As we go through life, it is a process of discovery as we learn what is possible from ourselves in difficult situations and interactions with others.

This process is simple—it is all about learning lessons. You do not need to overanalyze this; it just happens. Often it is our guides who plant the seeds that set up experiences in our life. The incidences, "coincidences," and dramas can be orchestrated by those in the spiritual dimension to further our growth and understanding. For example, we can be pushed into situations where it is necessary to find courage and strength that we do not think we have. When the lesson is over, we are changed forever and now have the experience and wisdom for sharing what we have learned and touching other lives.

As mentioned, this assistance is always given out of their love for us, and in no way is it ever intended to be harmful. Those who watch over us know our capabilities as we are faced with these life challenges. As Spirit knows our abilities, our own higher self guides us into situations that bring out our potential to be greater than we believe. This process expands us and touches us in ways we sometimes could not have even imagined beforehand.

Some experiences in our life can release subtle painful memories held deep within our subconscious. These memories usually come from events in our current life or even from past lives, as some such as Dr. Brian Weiss suggest.[1] Once these whisperings from former times are brought to light, we have a greater opportunity to examine them and work through them. This new understanding can assist us in moving forward with greater freedom and creativity to fulfill our purpose in life.

Knowledge may also come from access to the Universal Mind during this life or our accessing this information before taking on a human existence. There are those who believe we have the intention to take on particular roles before incarnating. Part of this process is being equipped with specific knowledge buried deep within our DNA, which then becomes active at the appropriate time in our lives when we take on the challenge we were meant to conquer.

## *Supportive Energy*

We all have spirit guides watching over us and may have a spirit "friend" who supports us with inspiration to help us in our work. Although we may not be consciously aware of this, our thinking is enhanced as we receive inspiration. In turn, we pass this on to others, creating a chain reaction that goes on geometrically.

If you are in a role to teach or inspire others, you may also receive extra assistance from the other side. If you are not aware of these energies consciously, you may experience them subconsciously while sleeping.

Did you ever wonder where some of the classical masterpieces of such brilliant musicians as Mozart or Beethoven came from? Or, have you wondered about the genius creativity of a Michelangelo, or some of the great artists in Hollywood

*Principle Six: The Orchestra behind the Scenes*

such as Steven Spielberg, or even fantastic inventors such as Einstein? Sure, these people have or had above-average abilities, but it is reasonable to believe they were also open to inspiration from spiritual influences either during sleep or the awakened state. We might say they were receptive to receiving ideas or creative influences from the Universal Consciousness that surrounds us all. Albert Einstein openly admitted to such a possibility more than once.[2]

Many people are, in fact, led by these energies, although they are not consciously aware of it. Mostly, we have smaller, subtle lessons in our daily lives that rarely catch our attention. If we happen to notice, we usually shrug off hard-to-believe situations as chance or coincidence, which feels mentally safer rather than believing that powers outside of ourselves may be operating simultaneously in cooperation with us.

Sometimes it is easier to recognize these signals when we are in deep trouble and have begun feeling helpless. We reach a point of surrender and our senses become heightened. Feeling desperate, we suddenly find inspiration and inner strength we never knew existed. For example, a person is lost and fighting for survival; certain death is approaching, and all of a sudden a miracle occurs and this individual is rescued. Too many explain such occurrences away as "luck," when in reality there can be many souls behind the scenes assisting in the outcome.

Let me emphasize again that the love and support that exist for each of us are incredibly deep and unconditional. They ultimately come from God and are often delivered by our guardian angels, who are always looking out for our best interests, even when this might not appear to us to be the case in difficult times.

## *Coincidences*

In my youth, a man said to me, "Luck is preparation for opportunity." There is some truth to this statement, as we sometimes make our own luck—through hard work we may create our own success. However, there are other times when chance and coincidence are just too good to be what is really going on.

How can you explain bumping into someone you were thinking about earlier in the day, when you have not seen the person in a long time? What are the chances you know who is calling when you hear the phone ring? Guides can send signals like this to nudge us in a particular direction. This is where "synchronicity" begins to take place . . . where people just "happen" to be in the right place at the right time. There is so much going on beyond our normal range of perception, and yet subconsciously we are all participating in this psychic space. ❧ *The reality is that we all are psychic, as we are all energy.* ❧ We all have God's light within us at varying levels depending on what we allow to come forth.

Ironically, what you think of as chance occurs as a direct result of your thoughts as they flow into the universe. ❧ *You are what you think and believe you are.* ❧ One could reference the "Law of Attraction"[3]—the philosophical idea that "like attracts like" and so we attract positive or negative situations based on our thoughts, attitudes, and beliefs—as one reason for coincidences, but there is another possible deeper explanation operating behind this law.

Your loved ones and guides on the other side know your thoughts, wants, and desires in life, and they will try to help you along your life journey. So, as you express a desire or thought to become more than you are, others in the heavenly realm will want to assist. Your intention as to why you desire something matters in this interaction and can offset the

## Principle Six: The Orchestra behind the Scenes

outcome of the situation. Integrity is most important when desiring help from the other side; it cannot be for personal gain or selfish reasons. Nor can the assistance be used to invade the privacy of another individual.

This does not mean you get everything you want; rather, you receive what is needed for moving you forward at that particular time. As your thoughts flow out from you, they are received by the spirit beings, and the next thing you know a so-called coincidence occurs. What seems like a random connection is sometimes arranged so that both parties may complete a communication. These communications become an exchange of energy or ideas—or even an apology—so one or both parties can let go of a problem and be free to continue on their life path.

While most people are unaware of the energy that surrounds us, intuitive people can often feel suddenly overwhelmed by sensory overload. As an intuitive, I can easily attest to this experience with people and even foods on a regular basis, as foods are energy too. For example, if you are sensitive to energy and you eat foods with a low-energy signature, you can feel awful after a meal. An example of a low-vibration food is one that is highly processed or loaded with preservatives. I recommend natural or organic foods as a staple in your diet, as they have a higher vibration, which contributes to overall better health. Foods can also retain the energy of the one who prepares it. For example, if the chef is very angry, some of that energy can remain with the food. The emotional energy that emanates from us travels in many directions. We are all multidimensional beings and receive impulses from a variety of sources.

Our relationship with those in heaven may appear complex, but it is rather simple. Our spirit guides and departed loved ones eagerly pave the way for us to grow and evolve. They show signs and signals heading us away from trouble, if we become aware. They want to see us living happy and fulfilling lives.

What's more, even if you had a difficult relationship with one or both parents during their life, when they pass over and review their life they may feel a need to assist you before your life is complete. If they are burdened with guilt or memories not representative of who they are striving to be now, they may feel that the energy between you and them must be rebalanced. Those in heaven want a clean slate so they can move forward in their own evolution.

This does not mean that it will be easy for any of us to notice these subtle offerings as they occur. Be aware of your gut feelings, your intuition, as this is a means of receiving information from your spirit guides. Occasionally, you may even hear thoughts from your own mind as a warning when in a dangerous or difficult situation. Pay attention—your spirit guide may sound like your own voice inside your head. When at rest, your mind will naturally be more open, aware, and receptive to the possibility of hearing or even feeling inspiration from this "orchestra behind the scenes," so anything you can do regularly to relax and quiet your mind will enhance your ability to make the most of the guidance you are receiving.

## The Yuwipi Ceremony

If you are one who goes to church, synagogue, or a religious temple wondering if your prayers are being heard, you should know there is a ceremony called a "Yuwipi" that can offer you a direct link to the Divine. This is a Native American Lakota healing ceremony that is held in high regard by its people. It is led by the tribe's spiritual leader, who early in life is groomed for such a role. This leader is also a "physical medium," one who lends his energy to enable spirits to cross over into our

## Principle Six: The Orchestra behind the Scenes

world to do physical things such as materialization in our dimension. This normally takes great energy on the part of a spirit, which is why you will rarely if ever see this.

When in this ceremony, however, one does not need to be clairvoyant or a medium to witness the materialization of a spirit. In fact, one of the things that makes this rite unique is that we are not required to have our psychic senses fully open to see the spirit guides come forward. They make their presence known for all to see. Spirit offers this visual gift because it believes their presence gives hope and helps convince others to believe in eternal life.

The tribe's medium undertakes this role for the purpose of emotional and/or physical healing for those in attendance at the ceremony and for proving that life is continuous beyond our physical bodies. Healing energy can also be sent to other people not present at the ceremony. This last statement is difficult for many people to understand. It works like this: since energy is all around us, we are—in essence—all connected. Thought is form of a finer vibration, and with *intention* the energy from the ceremony is sent out to those who need healing.

There is tremendous love and selfless energy being shared in the Yuwipi ceremony by the spiritual leader in an effort to help those in need. The same can also be said for those beings from the spirit world who come to this ritual to help those in the physical dimension who pray for people who need support. Spirits can provide guidance, healing, and love for those praying at the ceremony.

The Yuwipi leader usually trains and dedicates his life for the purpose of being a link or energy conduit between the Divine (Spirit and its helpers) and those in attendance at the ceremony. The Native Americans—at least those who follow the indigenous ways—do not think like white people or any modern people of another race. They live their lives in congruence with nature's energy and that of Earth. They possess great brotherly love for each other within their family and their own tribe. It is this genuine love and respect that many Native Americans hold in their hearts that helps them build a bridge to the spiritual realm. It is natural for them to act as conduits for spiritual energy.

In my spiritual journey, I have been privileged to witness firsthand the Yuwipi ceremony. The first time I attended one, I witnessed a whistle fly by me and a rattle shake by itself in thin air. I thought I was going to pee in my pants! I could never have believed this had I not seen it with my own eyes. Now, at least eight Yuwipi ceremonies later, I have felt a hand materialize, touch me, and then vanish into nothingness. I have seen other so-called impossible things, or what others might refer to as "miracles," occur as well. Oddly enough, the Lakota Indians attending this ceremony are hardly fazed by anything that takes place. Other people who are more scientific minded, such as myself, need a boatload of evidence to believe anything other than what we were taught in school—that "what you see is what you get."

In case you ever attend a Yuwipi ceremony, I want to emphasize that one does not need to be spiritually gifted or in optimal health to experience its energy and healing. I personally know a few people whose vitality was low—they were either near death or extremely emotionally depleted—who were strengthened from this ceremony. The experiences and results will differ among attendees, depending on their ailments and what is being healed. Obviously, there are no guarantees, but the healing and the love generated from this prayer ceremony are strong.

*Principle Six: The Orchestra behind the Scenes*

## Everyone Needs a Coach

If it is still a stretch for you to accept the idea that we are being continuously aided in our evolution by beings in the nonphysical dimension, perhaps you can think of it this way: even the best ball players in the world have a coach, so why not ourselves? Sometimes our "coaches" see things from afar that we miss or take for granted up close. And the people in heaven that may be watching over us have been this way before. They walked upon Earth before we did and accumulated life experience, making them suitable for the role of "guide." I personally find it very reassuring when I consider the intricately designed "orchestra" of which both we and our friends in heaven are a significant part.

CHAPTER 10

# PRINCIPLE SEVEN:

# Your Thinking Equals Your Experience

> *I am convinced that life is 10 percent what happens to me and 90 percent how I react to it.*
> —Charles Swindoll, goodreads.com

I always thought the expression "We are all characters and the world's a stage" was amusing, but I never thought of it in literal terms until, in my own evolutionary process, I came to understand that life is continuous. Ironically, the idea that the world as a stage is closer to the truth than you might believe.

We all play roles while we are here in this life. Some of our positions are intentional, as we are aware of our goals from day to day and actively go after them. Yet, some of us go about our lives caught up in the minutia, afraid of what may happen next—we sort of "happen into" our roles instead of creating them.

When you look back on your life, it will have layers and layers of experiences with people, places, and things. There will be lessons learned through these interactions that hopefully have brought clarity and wisdom where previously it had been lacking.

We all create our personal worlds that we live in as our path unfolds from day to day. These miniworlds are the realities in which we have chosen to participate. Others may take part in our particular "drama," or in some cases we may be essentially solitary and perhaps even lonely. One thing is for sure, though: we often think we are choosing our reality intentionally, based on our upbringing, learned behaviors, and experiences, only occasionally leaving things to chance.

Even if we believe we are living our lives randomly or allowing others to make decisions for us, there is an element of choosing this personal condition. This is the path we make for ourselves until something else comes along that forces us to take note. If we allow someone else to plan out a life for us, this is a reality we have accepted. Either we live our life with intention, or we end up living the choices of someone else. There is no judgment around this; it just often happens this way.

You may have a wish to make changes in your life but feel fearful or powerless to do so. If so, you are again living this particular reality. In other words, not making a decision is, in fact making a decision to stay where you are. How you think, how you feel, how you respond all manufacture the life you live. You define your experience with others and form the life you end up leading throughout your time here on Earth.

As important a distinction as this is for many to consider, I do not want to deemphasize that some people may have chemical imbalances, physical brain disorders, and true mental illness, which do not allow them to be fully in charge of their lives. This writing does not apply in these cases, as these are challenges of another kind.

Experiences often are not "good" or "bad" in and of themselves; they are just labeled this way by our thinking, beliefs, and attitudes, which are shaped by our upbringing and society. We attach feelings and memories to experiences, giving them

*Principle Seven: Your Thinking Equals Your Experience*

a life of their own. ❧ *If your thoughts are of violence, you become angry and violent; if you think love, you become lovingly and compassionate; if you worry all the time, you become anxious; if you are constantly jealous, you become resentful; if you think with imagination, you become creative; if you think happy thoughts, then you feel joy; if you think the glass is always half empty, you become cynical; if you think all people are bad, you wind up alone. Your choice of thinking determines how you create your experiences. Ultimately, it becomes the reality you make for your life. You can choose.* ❧

Depending on your upbringing, it may be more natural for you to use your imagination or your thinking processes in your approach to life. The discipline of your thoughts comes down to the focus of your mind and will power. Meditation, quiet time, and a suggestion before bedtime are all ways for moving oneself in a particular direction and thinking pattern. Confirms motivational speaker Zig Ziglar, "Evidence is conclusive that your self-talk has a direct bearing on your performance."[1]

Your reactions result from your thinking. Our feelings and emotional behaviors will sprout from the thoughts to which we give power. We are flesh and blood with positive qualities, vices, and automatic habits that reflect our inner ways and emotional needs. "Your habits today will determine your future," explains minister Joel Osteen. "Examine your life, take inventory of your behaviors, and when you find something that's not right, be quick to change."[2]

Try being flexible in your thinking and be willing to find new ways of being, matching your behavior with your ideals. Your mind creates the spark from which everything else follows. Emotions follow thought, and behavior follows emotions. Adding discipline to your thoughts may help you reach new heights in life, with a greater capacity to focus on your goals.

If nothing else, though, it may help you emotionally to avoid getting into trouble.

Following is an example of how this works: a sports team, thinking it is invincible, creates positive energy and strong thought forms, which in turn create uplifting emotion and enthusiasm both within the team and among its supporters. This is why many teams play better when they are at their home field or arena. The positive energy from a comfortable surrounding is uplifting. This is common, and you can now understand it from an energy perspective.

Thoughts have energy, and those that have been infused with emotion become "charged energy" that is visible to those who are clairvoyant (able to see energy in the form of auras, spirit guides, and images). This goes for thoughts that are negative and fearful as well as positive. It is all out there to be seen and felt by others. This is also why other people's emotions and behaviors are contagious and have influence on those around them, for good or ill. This process is subtle, yet powerful.

Many personal self-help coaches talk of the benefits and power of positive thinking. This is intentional, as the Bible verse from Matthew 7:7 affirms: "Ask and it shall be given you; seek, and you shall find; knock, and it shall be opened unto you."[3] What you think you are, you are. What you expect, you become. Remember what Edgar Cayce once said: "Spirit is the life, mind is the builder, and physical is the result."[4] The key phrase here is "mind is the builder"—where you focus your mind with *intention* is where you will go in life.

*The Power of Positive Thinking*, by Norman Vincent Peale, has sold millions since its first publication several decades ago. He recommends having belief and faith in yourself and faith in God. These are important attributes for moving yourself in a positive direction in life. They create a framework from which to work.

*Principle Seven: Your Thinking Equals Your Experience*

To take it one step further, there is already a piece of God in you—your soul, or subconscious and the luminous body within you that is divine energy. When you are thinking positive, loving thoughts, you give power to this energy in your body. You become the driver and can direct this force with your thoughts, your spiritual practices, and the way you choose to live your life. Says Dr. Carl Jung, "Your destiny is the result of the collaboration between the conscious and the unconscious."[5] It is not one being more important than the other; they work in tandem, taking you through the vast experiences life offers.

## *Control Your Mind, Control Your Life*

As your current thoughts create your current reality, your past experience and what you have been taught provide a platform from which your present thoughts arise. It can be a circle. Your prior experience influences your thoughts, promoting the manifestation of similar experiences again. This is why it is hard to break bad habits and have the discipline for making difficult decisions for change. You desire change for the better, but you hold back because your previous learned behaviors are still in the back of your mind, and these old habits are very entrenched. This is where discipline comes in; it helps to reinforce the thought "The past does not equal the future,"[6] expressed by self-help coach Tony Robbins.

Robbins also speaks of people's behavior patterns as they are motivated by pain or pleasure; he says many will do things to avoid pain and embrace pleasure in their lives. Yet preceding these behavior patterns and desires is the initial thought process and your decision for choosing which thoughts to embrace and which to discard. You can still *consciously* choose which direction to follow and supersede previous blueprints.

You always have the power for choosing which thoughts you give power to and which ones you put back in the vault. We all have had experiences that generate positive or negative feelings when we have been confronted with a brand-new situation. We all have had various occurrences and upbringings that contribute to our way of being. Still, even if it is not necessarily consciously, we choose on some level to be angry when disappointed or miserable when all alone. But there is another alternative: we have the option of not giving power to those thoughts, knowing there is something better around the corner. It is always a choice, an attitude, and then a decision. Motivational speaker Wayne Dyer speaks to this when he states: "With everything that has happened to you, you can either feel sorry for yourself or treat what has happened as a gift. Everything is either an opportunity to grow or an obstacle to keep you from growing. You get to choose."[7]

We are the creators of our own reality. Our reactions to various circumstances say a lot about who we are. Whether we like it or not, the world takes these reactions and judges us. It is human nature to label; slotting others in a particular category makes us feel safe, thinking we know more than we actually do about them. We falsely believe we are limiting the unpredictability of our environment and the world around us by labeling.

Here is an example of our power to respond to our situation positively or negatively: Three men are walking up a steep hill in winter to eventually sled down. As they near the top the first man says, "Oh my God, this hill is killing my legs; I cannot go any farther. Are we almost there?" The second man says, "Hey, this is great exercise; I have not had any time to go to the gym." The third man, smiling even though he is limping badly, says, "My knee is in pain, but I can't wait to fly down that hill."

This scenario shows three completely different ways of being

## Principle Seven: Your Thinking Equals Your Experience

and responding, even though all the men are experiencing the same event. The appearance of going up the hill seems to be the same for all three, yet each sees it from his own perspective. If you speak with each man separately, you will likely hear about three unique experiences going up the same hill. What makes the difference? It is the thought process each chooses to embrace and how each one reacts uniquely to the same set of criteria. Each man brings a different set of life circumstances that fosters a thinking pattern. Fundamentally, we are all responsible for our own thoughts and how we react to various circumstances. In the long run the choice is up to us.

When I first started out in business, I attended a seminar on selling. During the presentation the speaker began talking about attitude and the difference this makes in so many areas of life. He spoke of a situation that would make most of us shudder. He described a young man in his early twenties, who was initially successful and then was in an accident and a fire that left him disabled and burned over half of his body. Yet this young man did not focus on the wheel chair and his scars. He continued about his business, helping other people along the way. He eventually got married and created a very affluent life for himself. How many of us would have the courage and discipline to march forward as if nothing had ever happened after such an experience?

This young man made a conscious choice to continue forming the reality and life he wanted. It is more than just having determination; there is a decision that occurs first . . . a belief that this is the way it will be. This is the power of our minds—the power we all have, if we make a conscious choice to embrace it. Excellence is a choice, a deliberate thought pattern resulting in repeated behaviors. Life goes by very quickly, and if we hope to avoid regrets when reaching the end, making intentional choices along the way is critical.

Modern cultures have developed schools, sciences, therapies, and even medicine to deal with one's emotions, but much less focus has been given to the *thoughts* that underlie them. In my partnership with those in the heavenly dimension, I have discovered that emotions usually arise as a *byproduct* of thought rather than the other way around; many have it backward. Author and motivational speaker Denis Waitley describes it this way: "Life is the movie you see through your own eyes. It makes little difference what's happening out there. It's how you take it that counts."[8]

If your focus is changed to zero in on your thoughts and why you choose to embrace particular ones of them that are causing you pain, you may begin to experience more healing. It is a conscious decision to think certain thoughts, and you can choose ones that are more empowering and health-producing for you. Only after the thought has materialized do the emotional and physical responses associated with it take root.

What has been discussed portrays human thinking and tendencies. At the same time, there are many who feel with open hearts as part of their decision-making process. They are not afraid to listen to the wisdom of their emotional nature. The soul will speak to and direct us through our heart as well as through our mind. We can listen to it or filter it out in favor of our own personal choices. Our preferences can be based on a wide variety of needs, desires, and simple pleasures. Some choices may be in alignment with our highest good, and some may not. As the Buddha so wisely reminds us, "It's better to conquer yourself than win a thousand battles."[9]

## *Framing*

So many of our thoughts and the realities we produce are from what we may call a "frame of reference." This is part of our

## Principle Seven: Your Thinking Equals Your Experience

experience, and it is also a bit broader. For instance, if you are living in a Middle Eastern country, then your frame of reference and the social mores and laws you live by might be quite different than if you live in New York City. And the structure and social patterns in China are different from those in Africa, and so on.

What one person finds acceptable and another distasteful may be traced back to one's upbringing and this frame of reference. Religion is a perfect example. These frames of reference or learned behaviors can be deeply rooted in a person to the point of accepting that these beliefs are "truth." The result is a rigid thinking pattern and an inability to adapt to certain situations. Too much of what you perceive may be identified or categorized as right or wrong, thereby closing you down to opportunities and other realities.

❧ *Life is about change. It is always changing and evolving as the flow of energy itself is continuous.* ❧ If you consciously acknowledge some of your belief systems as "just a frame of reference," you become open to new possibilities. You can become more flexible in your thinking, more tolerant of others, and overall more in tune with the universe. On the other hand, digging your heels in when someone else does not share your religious beliefs pushes people away from you, and there is little possibility for relationship. Which approach better serves you and others?

The idea is for you to be *open* to what comes your way. You may not always know when opportunity comes knocking, and it could look different from what you were expecting. This is sometimes the way heaven works, and you need flexibility in your thinking to be receptive to what possibilities cross your path.

## Seeking Peace

At the deepest level, it is peace in one form or another that humanity strives for; even the warrior fights in the belief that this will bring him peace in some way. Yet what if this thought—that peace can be achieved by an action "out there"—is an illusion and you can find a way to locate peace within? Let me tell you that you can—the energy with which you came into this life is coded for something special. We all have gifts waiting to be expressed. As we search within ourselves and allow our divinity to come forth, harmony will ensue and we may find peace.

Many of us are warriors by day in our interactions with one another. Walking down the streets of New York City or running through Grand Central Station is proof enough to me that people have armor on. Sure, there may be a friendly chap here and there, and everyone's favorite hot dog vendor, but many are quick to judge and find fault with one another rather than see what they might share in common.

Connecting to our higher source and to the light that burns brightly within all of us can bring balance and harmony to our relationships. When we know that we are not alone and that we really have nothing to fear, there is a sense of peace that comes over us . . . a calmness that infuses every cell in our body. Things that may normally upset us have less of a negative effect and begin falling away. We know we can pick up and continue with whatever we were doing before the particular challenging circumstance entered our life. This type of experience is well within our reach; we just need to have the intent to occupy this space.

Energy flows as the current in a river, and the trick is to go with this flow of life. I am not saying to be a patsy and lie down when things are difficult. What is suggested is to be open to

*Principle Seven: Your Thinking Equals Your Experience*

embracing spiritual growth and, as a result, being receptive to the lesson that is being presented to us rather than avoiding it.

There's a lesson to be learned in nearly everything in life. If your circumstances suddenly become extraordinarily challenging, rather than resist, step back and ask yourself why this is so and evaluate what is happening. If you are out of step with the direction your life is heading, you may keep undergoing the same lesson until you truly understand it; this is your soul's way of getting your attention. Then sometimes you may experience this lesson in different forms until you change. That's the way the divine influences help you progress.

When you begin to understand how much you are loved and cared for by helpers on the other side, you may be more apt to chuckle or laugh when things get out of sorts. Try having faith in a higher power that knows who you are and trust the process. And going through it with a peaceful heart will likely help you to move through the challenges more quickly.

## *Global Coming of Age*

When we understand how our thinking defines our experience and the reality we make for ourselves, perhaps we can decide as a civilization what reality to live by. For example, it appears that money is often worshiped more than people or those we claim to care about, and this defines our choices in ways that benefit the few rather than the many. We are on this Earth for a very short time, and if we are to gain wisdom and understanding, we need to adjust our priorities.

For centuries humanity has had to meet the challenge of sustenance in one form or another. Since the Industrial Revolution, many parts of the world have conquered this issue to some degree. Accumulation has become the focal point in modern times. And too often it is accumulation at all cost, which leaves many by the wayside. Now that the human race dominates all other species on this planet, the concept of survival of the fittest seems to be applied toward one another. We need to move much more in the direction of cooperation than competition. Ideally, for the human race to advance we must get rid of hatred, violence, and the desire for power.

The accumulation phase is bringing us to an inflection point where the mechanisms in place for supporting our needs are being stretched to their capacity. At what point is it enough? The focus of accumulation distracts and falsely directs us away from the prime reasons why we incarnate, which are to experience lessons of learning and wisdom, and to be of service to each other and to our planet.

There have been times in history where there have been tipping points and nations have had an opportunity for traveling in multiple directions. America's choice to engage in World War II and even its war for independence are two such examples that could have dramatically changed the world's history, had a decision been made to submit to an aggressor rather than fight for freedom. Sometimes, countries have chosen well and humankind has moved forward, and at other times our disregard for the value of human life has led to wars and bloodshed.

We are in a time when the human spirit is being challenged. The choices we make as a society will be felt for many years to come. Our focus must change from self to each other, and this applies to the global community as well.

This is a time for taking inventory of our purpose and what we want from life as individuals and a civilization . . . beyond material needs and what our egos perceive they need to feel satisfied. It is a time to reach out and help others in need. Whether we admit it or not, many of us need emotional healing in one form or another, and we need this healing from other people; money does not do this. As we heal, our hearts naturally open

## Principle Seven: Your Thinking Equals Your Experience

more and become an empowering source of support for others. This sets an example and becomes an opportunity for others to see and emulate the loving, unifying behavior.

The world is run by many "accumulation worshippers." They believe that material gain and wealth are the most important things that define who we are. This is very far from the truth—when material gain is how you define yourself, your self-concept can easily be torn down.

☙*All that matters is what is within your heart; this is what God sees.* ☙ If your life is filled with love, it doesn't matter how many possessions you have. Love is true currency and something that can be shared and passed on to others. ☙*As others receive your love, it shifts them closer to their purpose and enables the love to be passed on again and again, creating a chain that gains more strength with each link that is added.* ☙ Eventually, this chain can circle the world over and over again.

Our Creator intended for us to live in peace and freedom so that we would be able to evolve. We are all part of the same Source, the original Soul that began long ago. It has given a piece of itself many times over in creating each of us. This is why it is said that we are all one. We are all the same under the cover of our various physical forms.

Many in the world, in the name of power and control, restrict human rights, even killing, torturing, and manipulating others for personal gain. Not only does this prevent those being hurt from fulfilling their destiny, it is a great setback for those using power irresponsibly. Nation upon nation rising with swords and, still worse, swords upon their own citizens spreads fear and hinders our ability to evolve as a civilization.

We as a global community have a responsibility to act together. Too often it is the same countries that get involved, such as the United States acting alone or with just a few other partners. All nations need to act in unison to stop the violence and bloodshed all over the planet, or it will keep popping up where it sees weakness.

Those who attain power are presented with an opportunity for personal growth as well as having a larger-scale impact to guide history. There are powerful leaders in countries throughout the world who can exercise their will and their ego and make decisions that impact millions of people. Mikhail Gorbachev, the former prime minister of the Soviet Union, put his ego aside and set an example for humanity by granting freedom to millions of people who were imprisoned by the Iron Curtain. Former Iraqi president Saddam Hussein was on the opposite end of the spectrum, and he paid for it with his life. Those who are leaders have the potential to further both individual and global evolution with the choices they make. How they deal with that responsibility is what is at stake here on a personal as well as a soul level.

Often it is fear that causes people to do horrible things they otherwise could never conceive of. Fear-motivated behavior goes on throughout the world and is used for justifying decisions, and these consequences affect many innocent people. Since everything is energy, the darker emotions of fear, violence, hate, anger, and desire for revenge can be passed to others as well as can specific physical actions.

Once in power, even initially well-meaning people often fear giving up control. We see it in a variety of circumstances in business and politics. We see it every day in larger settings with leaders of countries. The atrocities that have been discovered throughout history are hard to even grasp. Too often it appears that some leaders have focused upon themselves and lost the ability to feel empathy or compassion for the people. In their greed to hold on to or expand their power, they lose their human kindness and respect for life as if they are above it all.

## Principle Seven: Your Thinking Equals Your Experience

The truth is that there really is nothing to fear, so all these fear-based actions are not necessary or productive. Human existence is a temporary state for learning and not our eternal, continuous identity. When we leave this material form, we return to the bigger part of who we really are. Fear fills us with a false identity; it takes over when we believe we are less than we are.

What you do and how you treat others is what you become—there is no escape. You cannot kill another person for personal gain and think you are not affected by this. You cannot then just expect to arrive home, tuck your baby in to sleep, and kiss your wife goodnight as if nothing had happened—who you are and what you have done will be felt by all those around you. Likewise, you cannot be a leader of a country making wholesale decisions to end others' lives and destroying families you feel are a threat, and then show up at the United Nations with a smile and a handshake, then return again to your country to use lethal force everywhere you see fit. In time, this behavior has its own repercussions. These decisions will follow you beyond this life, and you will ultimately have to make amends to all you have wronged. As Russell Crowe, in the role of Maximus Decimus Meridius in the movie *Gladiator*, so well expressed, "What we do in life echoes in eternity."[10]

We are not the first civilization to inhabit this planet; it is widely accepted by historians and scientists that there were others who lived here long before us. One of these was Atlantis, which thrived around twenty-five thousand years ago. It seems the Atlanteans misused their power and this led to disaster. Some of their history is now underwater, and what is left of their culture made its way long ago to Central America, Europe, and the Middle East.[11]

We cannot continue on like this, and the Creator, God, Allah, Source—whatever label you have for your Maker—is saying, "Enough!" We need to change or changes will be made for us. It is our problem to rectify *now*, not leave it to others down the road to deal with. It is our responsibility to make things right.

Our deeds in life count towards eternal progress. On the other hand, sitting too often as an observer may hinder your development and has never helped anybody. We are put on this Earth to be useful and help one another.

Regardless of your circumstances, the life you have is a blessing, and it and everything around you must be treated with care. Chad Kroeger, a songwriter for the Nickelback rock group, addresses this idea in Nickelback's song, "If Today was Your Last Day."[12]

This song expresses that each day of life is a gift and should not be taken for granted. We should not be afraid to go out into the world and make our mark. And it suggests that if you did not have much time left perhaps it should be spent mending a broken heart.

Try asking this question of yourself: If you had only one week to live, how would you treat everyone around you? Would it be very different from how you normally are? Would you suddenly be appreciating things a little more? Your responses can become a guidepost for how you live your life *right now*. Maybe there are some changes that need to be made, people you need to acknowledge, and others to whom you could open your heart. Attempt this idea and see how freeing this can be from your ordinary range of thinking and doing.

### *You Can Decide*

It is true some people are dealt a different hand of cards at birth. You may be born into poor rural circumstances or a rich urban family, but the choices you make along the way will

*Principle Seven: Your Thinking Equals Your Experience*

determine how your story unfolds—it is not an accident that people may find themselves in prison or running for election as a US senator. The reality we create in life is based on a multitude of decisions that form layer upon layer of experiences, shaping our existence. Our thoughts influence what occurs in our outer world, so constantly monitoring our inner beliefs and attitudes will help match them to the experience in life we are seeking. And, being willing to shift them as necessary to move with change is an important personal practice for us all.

However, sometimes in life we do not get to choose, but rather we must make the most of what we are given—this becomes our personal opportunity to evolve from that point on. In the end, it is always our thinking that defines our experience.

PART FOUR

# It Starts with You

*There is no passion to be found playing small, in settling for a life that is less than the one you are capable of living.*
—Nelson Mandela, briantracy.com

CHAPTER 11

# THE JOURNEY WITHIN

> *Don't let the noise of others' opinions drown out your own inner voice. And most important, have the courage to follow your heart and intuition.*
>
> —Steve Jobs, goodreads.com

We have all heard that a long journey starts with the first step. In this case, it is your first step on a journey of discovery. Searching within is the beginning of drawing closer to the purpose of why you are here. Discovering your light—your soul that dwells within and your spiritual connection to God—is the next frontier coming in human evolution. The mainstream population will learn what some mystics and Native Americans have always known: that we are not alone on this journey of life.

### Everyone Is an Enlightenment Center

If you are able, even if only for one brief moment, to look, your answers are always within. While you may know this on some level, maybe you are afraid of what you might hear or feel. However, this is just your emotional/intellectual self (ego) talking, not your essence. Your choices and decisions are not always easy ones to make, and you want to make them with the best resources available to you. Listening to your inner wisdom with an open heart is essential to living authentically.

Individually, each of us is a key for unlocking the great divine energy that permeates us all. As one key turns, many others will follow; together we can move closer to the truth that is meant for each of us. No man or woman is ever an island unto him- or herself; those who suffer in loneliness or depression, for example, must come to know that if they reach out there is a guiding hand to clasp theirs.

There may be no greater pursuit than the freedom to be who we were meant to be so that each of us may fulfill the purpose for which we have come into this world. Yet many choose a life that appears to contradict this possibility. Perhaps this happens unintentionally, as most of us are unaware of the gifts we possess and are meant to develop while we are here, but it can also occur deliberately, out of discomfort with what it may feel like to be different or be criticized. You have the freedom to choose the path you wish to take in this life.

When starting my spiritual journey, I reconsidered what and who I had been up to that point. I was forced to ponder some of the usual questions we face, as well as those we refuse to explore out of fear of the unknown. While I had no particular spiritual or religious belief system guiding my life, I had an open mind. And an open mind is one that is flexible and has the ability to consider things outside the normal framework of what we are programmed to think.

Sometimes, there is a lack of listening to one's inner voice, which is begging to be heard. How many times do we have this intuition, or "gut feeling," and ignore it in favor of our desires or what others are telling us we should do? The inner source, or soul, is one of a divine nature that is propelled by love. Trusting our deeper feelings and inner voice is a key for moving us forward on our path. This internal mechanism is waiting to be tapped and will lead us to a closer relationship with heaven and the Divine. As more people draw closer to those in the spiritual dimensions, it will help form a brotherhood of man, which is sorely lacking. Together we will move toward hope, unity, and peace and away from disillusionment, disconnection, and discord.

## Seven-Step Process for Spiritual Expansion and Healing

Part of being equipped to bridge the worlds of the physical and the spiritual realms is going within yourself and clearing the emotional and mental pathways for your own energy to flow. Becoming centered and more grounded helps provide a good foundation for developing your psychic senses and working with the heavenly realm.

1. Put aside your doubts and be open to possibilities. An open mind is a powerful receptor.
2. Understand the connection between mind, emotions, body, and soul. If one of these areas is out of alignment, it short-circuits the connection and power they have together. Strive for harmony of being.
3. Learn to tame and manage your outward and inward feelings, recognizing how you express emotion in order to hear the voice of a greater power, love.
4. Be authentic; be true to yourself. Know there is a higher power that loves you unconditionally for who you are and wants you to love yourself and others.
5. Learn to meditate, and then do it regularly. Quiet the body so you can focus the mind with intention. Your

mind is not your brain, it is not part of your body, it is not limited to the physical boundaries of your body, and it will exist even after the death of your body.

6. Join or create a spiritual development Circle with others where you can practice meditation, raise your energy vibration, conduct psychic exercises, and expand spiritual awareness.

7. Trust this process and those in the heavenly realm. Have faith in a higher power.

The tools given here, if followed, will lead you to a new relationship with yourself and a much greater expression of the true reason you are here. Says the teacher White Eagle, in *Spiritual Unfoldment 1*, "The fundamental purpose of your life is that you may find truth, truth which will be unveiled to you by your own inner self. As we search for this truth which lies buried deep within, the barriers erected by the outer self will vanish and we shall become free."[1]

## Tuning In to Your Higher Self

When life traumas occur, the conscious mind (ego) begins to slow down, and your higher self, or soul, steps in and begins to lead. This deeper part of you is always there, but it is too often overshadowed by your personality and your mind's racing thoughts. If you are in a deeply relaxed state or a meditative state of being, your deeper soul-self may come through most willingly with wisdom and purpose.

It does not matter what your social status is or what you have or have not accomplished in life, the formula is always the same: search within as a method of guidance to drawing you closer to your inner voice, the voice of Spirit within you.

In the midst of our busy lives, this voice is barely audible, but when we are quiet and still, as in meditation, there is a greater chance that we may hear it. If it does not show up for you as an audible voice, it may come as an inspiration or an idea upon initially waking up from sleep. Remain completely still, between deep sleep and being fully awake, and you may notice this inspiration from the dream state or feel it within as an emotion. If you get up too quickly, you will likely miss it and forget your dreams.

Even if you do not hear or feel anything at first, with practice you will begin to notice this inner prompting. It may sound like your own voice or thoughts coming from another place—a higher soul-self or even a spirit guide offering an idea. People experience this all the time and do not realize that the voice is coming from somewhere else, directed from a different plane of existence.

Sitting quietly and observing your own thoughts during meditation, with the intention to relax and be still, begins to calm the active mind. This allows the process to unfold in time, and inner guidance may rise from the depths of your soul. The more active your conscious mind is in general, the more time you may need for this spiritual practice. Be patient with yourself. It took me two years of weekly commitment before this made any sense to me.

Interestingly, going deep into one's mind is a personal exploration that is as new and exciting as exploring a wilderness. You never know what may come up for you in reflection or a meditation. The mind and your subconscious are similar to the concealed oceans of Earth. This realm is beautiful and mysterious, and much is hidden from plain sight. It is a real journey into the unknown. Even more fascinating is that this unknown is the authentic you. Most people never take the time for this spiritual practice and are unaware of the deeper parts of themselves.

It is important to emphasize that the process of self-discovery is not linear and will vary from person to person; the journey is personal and different for each of us. How we use our senses and respond to the information that is revealed to us is unique as well. A common experience, though, is coming out of this practice with more of a connection to your own soul—being reminded of who you really are. Essentially, you are relearning what you buried deep within your subconscious mind before you incarnated. You are more powerful than you can imagine—a divine being who is here for a purpose.

Do not be concerned if you are not yet aware of your purpose. Bishop T. D. Jakes gives this advice: "If you can't figure out your purpose, figure out your passion. For your passion will lead you right into your purpose."[2] It will lead you where you need to be even if it is only a temporary lesson on your life path. Taking it a step further, Esther and Jerry Hicks in their *Law of Attraction Journal* say that you have free will and that when your will begins reflecting the Creator's will, you will find harmony.[3]

## *Methods for Raising Your Energy Vibration*

When you are able to cast off your lower instincts and earthly minds in favor of heart-based thoughts, you are moving in the right direction. It is not an easy process to become lighter in frequency and vibration, but it is worth every moment devoted to this task. (See Appendix B for an exercise to assist in evaluating your energy centers to raise your vibration.)

Most of us do not have the time or the desire to work on ourselves with intentions of making self-improvements. Some feel they are already successful and have everything they need. Others have personal belief systems that may not allow for thinking we have a spiritual power within that is ready to be unleashed when called upon. Many disbelieve that we can actually take control of our destiny, as life has us tightly boxed in. In other cases, we have been told how to act, how to think, and what will or will never be. Out of fear or a lack of self-worth, we falsely believe that this is our truth.

All of these patterns and thinking are self-induced—they are not handed down from Source, from God. We are our worst enemies with negative self-talk. I had many of these patterns myself before embarking on my own awakening, so I know it is possible to create new, more empowering thoughts and, thus, ways of being.

Everything is energy that vibrates at a frequency. In beginning your journey of self-discovery and awakening, you will want to embrace higher vibrations in life and avoid or reduce those patterns of low vibration. Emotionally, love and gratitude are expressions of the highest vibration and frequency, while anger and fear are low vibrations.[4] As human beings we express many emotions and it is healthy to release them, but the question is, what do we want our life to be like? We have the power to impact this positively or negatively.

If your circumstances are undesirable, consider stepping back mentally and emotionally to see things from all perspectives. This may help you to remain neutral. Try viewing your predicament first as a learning opportunity rather than reacting with anger or violence. "Turn stumbling blocks into stepping stones and the rest will be given,"[5] counsels Edgar Cayce. ◈ *Put down your sword, be more patient, pray for change, and see what happens.* ◈ Action as violence should always be a very last resort and, even then, only in self-defense.

What follows are several methods to help you physically change your state of being so you may increase your energy vibration and function optimally physically, emotionally, mentally, and spiritually. We are all individually unique, and you will find that some methods resonate with you better than others.

*Diet*

Eat healthy foods. What you put in your body has an energy vibration that resonates with a frequency. Not surprisingly, fruits and vegetables have a higher vibration than sugar and alcohol. Foods that are highly processed with preservatives are also of a lower vibration. People disagree as to whether eating meat is an issue affecting one's energy vibration and ability to work with those in the heavenly realm. I personally have not seen any meat eaters who had difficulty working with non-physical beings.

In my own experience, many times after consuming foods with preservatives I lacked energy or had migraine headaches. Sometimes, I was sick until the food passed through my system. Common sense should prevail when it comes to what you put in your body. This also means no recreational drugs and limiting alcohol to social situations or in moderation; those in the heavenly realm will not work with you if you have drugs or alcohol in your system. Eating too many sweets and getting high on sugar will also drain your energy resources until your body regains its balance.

*Sound*

There are scientific studies that suggest that everything in the universe, including our bodies, is made up of vibrational sound.[6] One study shows how a water molecule changed its pattern based on the sounds to which it was exposed. Likewise, as human beings we can change our emotional state when listening to music. The vibrational energy of sound offers a way to calm the mind, quiet the body, and allow the troubles of the day to fall by the wayside. Depending on your choice of music, it may have a calming or uplifting effect. Higher vibrational sounds, such as classical music, can help align and balance energy centers within the human body and aura. Even rock 'n' roll music can raise energy levels through your lower-chakra energy centers.

Music touches one's soul and can speak in a unique language that other forms of sound and communication cannot. Yet, what resonates with one person may not have the same effect on another. We have our own preferences or perhaps we like to listen to what our soul needs to vibrate at its optimum frequency.

You can purchase CDs and DVDs that offer specific sounds and tones corresponding to the seven chakras in the human body. While listening to these sounds it is best to be sitting quietly in a meditative state, so you can most effectively soak up all the vibrations that resonate with your centers. This type of meditation in time will help balance and open some of your chakras.

Companies such as Hemisync and a few others have such programs available for this purpose. Sounds that produce vibrational tones in alpha and theta brain waves will help you reach a deeper meditative state. If you live near a metaphysical center or store, there are Tibetan or crystal singing bowls for purchase that also produce tones that will help balance and open your energy centers; there are CD recordings available of these tones as well.

Tuning forks also come in many varieties and are able to produce sound waves that correspond to the chakras in the human energy field. Working with a practitioner who understands frequencies of tuning forks can enable you to balance your chakra energies and even help you reach deeper meditative states.

## Meditation

While music changes your emotional state, meditation quiets the mind and places the body at rest. I learned from experience that if you meditate regularly, you will find more clarity in your thoughts and a general calming of your state of being. Should you be meditating with a purpose—such as modifying your own behavior for releasing emotional blocks and becoming one with the Creator—in time you will see small changes begin to occur. These changes will be different for everyone.

It is important to be patient with yourself. To begin, try meditating a few times a week, if not every day, for at least fifteen minutes; over time, if desired, you can gradually increase your duration. If you need the discipline of other people, you might join a local meditation group. You might find some "Meetups" online where like-minded people meet for this purpose.

There are also meditation CDs available for purchase. If you do not meditate regularly, following along with these guided meditations can be a great way to start your practice. The Edgar Cayce Society (A.R.E. in Virginia) has many meditation CDs and DVDs. The Sounds True publishing company also produces numerous meditation CDs, such as those by Jack Kornfield and other spiritual teachers.

### Color Meditation for Opening Your Energy Centers for Spiritual Work

The power of breathing through meditation cannot be underestimated. With intention, you can raise your energies through breathing. With intention, you can slow your breathing down with deep breaths and move yourself into a state of relaxation. This brings your body to rest, but not to sleep. Place your focus on the exhale, making sure your exhale is longer and deeper than the inhale. You will feel more relaxed as you begin letting go of any stresses that you carry with you from day to day. Using your breath to let go is an excellent way to prepare yourself before any meditation.

Following is a meditation that I have found very beneficial that uses imagination and the energy of different colors to assist in opening the chakras.

*To begin, sit quietly in a chair, with your eyes closed, your palms up, and your feet flat on the floor. Take a few deep breaths, focusing on the outflow. With each outflow, let go and feel yourself moving deeper into relaxation. (Do this for about thirty seconds.)*

Now, imagine your feet growing down into and through the floor, grounding you with Mother Earth. Imagine a bright white light coming down from above, embracing you, washing away any tears or fears, and protecting you with pure love.

See yourself standing on a beach at the edge of the surf on a beautiful, inviting summer day. As the warm ocean water comes in, it gently flows over your ankles, beginning to embrace you with Earth's energy. And with each wave and each breath, you are letting go more and more. You begin noticing the sounds of the waves and the seagulls flying overhead.

You look down in the water and see a red rock in the sand. You begin to feel the red energy from this rock go up through your feet up to your first energy center, at the base of the spine. Your first chakra opens.

You look down again and see an orange starfish in the sand. You begin to feel the orange energy of the starfish enter your feet and move up to your second energy center, the sacral. Your second chakra opens.

You look again in the water below and see a yellow sea shell. You feel its yellow energy entering your feet and flowing up your legs, as it finds its way to the third energy center, at your solar plexus. Your third chakra opens.

As you feel your first three chakras open, you look out onto the horizon and begin noticing the beautiful emerald-green color of the ocean before you. This emerald-green energy enters your feet and rushes up to your fourth energy center, in the area of your heart. Your fourth chakra opens.

Direct your gaze up at a gorgeous blue sky. The color blue enters your feet and moves up through the first four energy centers to your fifth, at the throat. Your fifth chakra opens.

You turn toward the beach and see some shellfish washed up on shore with the color indigo trickling out of their shells. You begin feeling the indigo energy coming up through your feet and running up to your sixth energy center, at the brow, between and just above your eyebrows. Your sixth chakra opens.

As you walk back up the beach, you notice a violet beach chair with white balloons placed there for you to sit down on. As you sit in this chair, the energy of the violet color begins to permeate you, moving up from your feet, through your first six energy centers, and up to your seventh center, at the top, or crown, of your head. The seventh chakra opens.

Now that all of your chakras are open and connected by energy, watch the white balloons detach from your chair. As they do so, all of your energy merges up through your crown, creating white light. Feel your energy move up from the base of your spine to your crown and back down again.

You are now open and ready to come back from your meditation to work in Circle. If you are not part of a Circle, then use this meditation at home or wherever you meditate.

*When you are finished with your spiritual work, remember to close down your energy centers. Starting at the crown and going in reverse order, just imagine closing each center with a door, finishing with the first chakra.* Then imagine pulling an imaginary zipper from the top of your energy field above your head, pulling in your energy field from all directions to the bottom of your feet. This allows you to finish your inner work before going on with your daily business.

### Yoga and Tai Chi

The practice of yoga and tai chi, both of which include movement of the body while focusing on the breath, can help shift us into a relaxed state of unification of mind, body, and spirit, which can result in raising our energy vibration. When done as yogis do it, through a focus on the breath (*pranayama*), yoga, which is in general more stationary, gently helps absorb the pranic, or "life force," energy in the air. In contrast, in tai chi, which is often described as "meditation in motion," with the constant movement of the body, practitioners feel as though they are grabbing the energy out of the air and pulling it into their own energy field. With intention and awareness, this power then finds its way to those chakras within the body where it is most needed and begins to flow more freely up and down all of them. With regular practice, yoga and tai chi help strengthen the body and increase energy that can be used for healing and spiritual work.[7]

### Prayer

One of the best methods for personal communication with the Source, the Great Spirit, God, or whatever term you use for the Creator is prayer. The experience of praying is very powerful. It lightens your mind, as you are turning your problems and concerns over to a higher power. Praying may help raise your energy vibration and supports your relationship with Spirit. Anything that raises your vibration brings you into closer attunement with the All.

Prayer by even one individual is worthwhile; prayer by many can lead to what some consider to be miracles. Even if you do not belong to a formal religious organization, I would encourage you to pray for a few moments each day with love and gratitude in your heart. Even a short prayer made early in the morning or before bed at night is heard by your angels and guardians on the other side. They will try to help if you make your wishes known.

## Dowsing

The ancient art for locating water, minerals, or other objects that seem to have a natural magnetic, electromagnetic, or other perhaps unknown energy is called "dowsing." Master dowser Walt Woods describes the dowsing process and how a beginner can use this methodology in his *Letter to Robin* (obtained through the American Society of Dowsers).[8] There are engineers today across the world who will resort to dowsing when their computers and fancy devices are unable to locate water in the ground.

When dowsing to locate water, a handheld device such as a Y-rod, L-rod, bobber, or pendulum is used. It is believed that the dowser uses one of these tools as a form of communication with his own subconscious, or higher self. By quieting the mind and becoming still, these devices will pick up sensitive vibrations and literally move on their own, providing an answer to the intended question. It is generally accepted by most dowsers that spiritual influences help to provide the energy to move the pendulum in an intended direction, supplying the dowsers with an answer to their question.

The pendulum is of particular importance, as it is most easily used by a beginner dowser. It is a basic tool with tremendous power if you learn to use it correctly. You must program the pendulum so you understand what information you are receiving when you are using it. The *Letter to Robin* is excellent reference material for understanding this process.

Master Dowser Sue Collins suggests using a dowsing "protocol" to help you achieve accurate responses.[9] In other words, you don't just pick up a pendulum and expect it to provide you with knowledge unless you first follow a number of steps beforehand. This suggested sequence speaks of clearing your own energy field, balancing energy in your physical body, and seeking permission from your higher self or spirit guide as some of the requirements before starting.

From practice, I can tell you that pendulum dowsing potentially enables everyday people, who are not yet advanced metaphysically, to work with their higher self and potentially their spirit guides. To have more accurate results, you must always be ethical and have the right intentions behind your questions.

## A Spiritual Circle: Working with Heaven

If you desire to develop your psychic awareness and expand your auric energy field, participation in a spiritual Circle is to me the most powerful way to do so. This involves a *collaboration* with forces beyond ourselves in addition to the more individualistic practices described above. Sitting in a Circle, as I was privileged to do for five years, is the best way for those in the heavenly realm to awaken the spirit and energy that dwell in each of us. While music, prayer, yoga, and meditation will help grease the wheels and stimulate our soul for personal growth, a Circle focuses our energy in a supportive environment, enabling us to unfold at our own pace. Also, the spiritual forces around us will use the group energy in the circle to assist each person's psychic development.

The shape of the Circle allows all participants to link their auras, which magnifies the intensity of the power each person would have alone. This helps individuals build their own energy for completing the exercises. This control is necessary if one wishes to work with those in heaven and be in service to help others. It takes great power to be able to form this bridge between our world here on Earth and our friends in the heavenly realm. And, it is actually the spirit guides who will deliver, over time, the expansion necessary to a person's aura, enabling an individual to communicate with the Divine.

In towns and cities across the globe you may be able to locate a spiritual Circle, such as the one in which I participated, to join. (See Appendix C for some locations where they are found.) A Circle, as we discussed earlier, is a group of like-minded people who meet each week for the purpose of expanding the spiritual gifts we all have. The practices done in a Circle help bring us into closer communication with our soul. It is important to note that a Circle does not take the place of one's religion or attending a church, mosque, or synagogue. Neither is a Circle right for everyone, especially not for those mentally handicapped or those physically ill.

## *Tips for Building a Successful Circle*

Following is a list of things I learned from my own experience that assist in achieving maximum benefit from working with others in a Circle:

1. Participants should meet on a weekly basis at the same time. It is assumed that all participants have a desire to enhance their relationship with the Divine and develop themselves in a way that they will be able to use their gifts to enrich their own life and be of service to others.

2. Be disciplined in your approach and in your exercises; you are working with divine energy.

3. There should be one who leads the group and oversees the meditations and exercises. This person should have advanced psychic senses or be metaphysically open to the energy around us.
4. There should be at least four or more participants—ideally six to ten—gathered in the shape of a circle. More people means more energy for the Circle.
5. Each participant must be of sound mind and free of any recreational drugs or alcohol.
6. People should not join a spiritual Circle to solve their emotional problems. Emotional issues may prevent you from working with the heavenly realm.
7. You must have patience with yourself and others—it takes a long time to develop your psychic senses.

A good spiritual Circle is based on trust, integrity, discipline, and support for each other in the group while helping you develop your energy awareness. If you find a Circle that is based on anything else, opt out. An effective Circle will offer meditation and exercises in intuition, and will assist you in raising your vibration, bringing you ever closer to the angelic realm and the Source of all creation.

We all have talents in this life, and one of the goals of a Circle is to help bring these abilities to the surface. Some people are highly intuitive, some are more mediumistic (able to communicate with those in the spiritual dimensions), and other people are natural healers. The energy we all have vibrates at different rates, and the frequencies are as distinctive as fingerprints.

Some children are born with these aptitudes open and functioning; however, if their parents offer no support, the children may shut down and their abilities will be buried deep within.

Nevertheless, these gifts remain as an essential part of their nature throughout their lifetime. The children may question themselves and not understand if their gifts begin to surface and reveal themselves once more.

An example might be people who have "second sight," which means that they see auras around people and/or begin to hear things that no one else can. These individuals may find themselves in conflict, confused, and feeling out of place without understanding why. Yet, in this situation, nothing is improper; they are exactly who God intended them to be. Their experience represents only the tip of the iceberg of what is possible and coming in the years ahead. We are on the verge of the "Age of Intuition," where the people of this planet begin to progress themselves to a place of enlightenment and a higher awareness of what reality is and why they are alive.

## Spiritualism

"Spiritualism" is a belief system that acknowledges the existence of an afterlife and that Spirit is a prime element of reality. It can be thought of as the religion of all religions, with its tenets that there is life after death, immortality, and the existence of God.[10] Historically, the Spiritualist movement began in 1848 in Hydesville, New York, when the Fox sisters, at home one evening, began hearing communication from those who had passed over into the spirit world. Growing in popularity from that first instance, for many years Spiritualism was the most prevalent form of religion or belief in the United States. Some very credible people acknowledged its value, as the following anecdotes reveal.

## *The Influence of Spiritualism on Abraham Lincoln*

Nettie Coburn, of Christian faith, was one of the great spiritual mediums of the nineteenth century in the United States and at a time when Spiritualism was generally accepted. In 1891 when she was terminally ill, she wrote her autobiography. In it Coburn states that although she had been sworn to secrecy and had kept some events hidden from public view, the information and experiences she had had were too important to take to the grave.[11]

Coburn had a friendship with a man working in the War Department who had an acquaintance with the first lady, Mary Lincoln. At this time in history, Mrs. Lincoln was open to Spiritualism, as were others in Washington. As Coburn became more known, in 1862 she was invited by Mrs. Lincoln to the White House. She was asked to lead a spiritual circle in the Red Room parlor, where President Lincoln himself stopped in to observe.

There was much on the president's mind with the Civil War going on, and he had been working on something we now know of as the Emancipation Proclamation. All his political advisers had been asking him to defer its enforcement or do away with it all together. However, the information Nettie Coburn brought forth from the heavenly realm urged the president not to abate its terms or delay the Emancipation Proclamation any longer. She also told him to stand firm in his convictions and fulfill the mission for which he had been raised. The president believed what he had heard, and the Emancipation Proclamation became the crowning event of his administration and his life.

Although attending a Circle was not a regular ritual for President Lincoln, he was so impressed with the information and knowledge Coburn had brought forward that she was asked again by Mary Lincoln to hold a Circle in the White House. It seemed that the war was not going well and morale was deteriorating, so the heavenly realm suggested that Lincoln himself go down to the front lines without generals and visit the men in regular clothes. He again acted on this suggestion, and the soldiers, seeing him not in his stately attire, came together and united once more.

There are so many facts and specific references to real people in Nettie Coburn's autobiography that one has to wonder why a dying woman, after thirty years of secrecy about these events, would be telling anything but the truth. It appears that potential judgment and ridicule could be the only reasons why such events have been all but written out of our history.

## The Remission and Resurgence of Spiritualism

Unfortunately, after the time of President Lincoln, as often happens with initially authentic practices, charlatans appeared and fraudulently began taking advantage of unsuspecting people. It became difficult to tell what was a real communication from those in heaven and what was make-believe because there were so many con artists posing as fake mediums. Eventually, people lost interest in this work and Spiritualism was replaced by other belief systems and religions.

Today, however, this trend is reversing itself, and many churches in England are based on Spiritualism. It has become one of the largest denominations of organized faiths, with healing Circles and Circles for spiritual development. (The Circle in which I have participated stems from this tradition.) The Spiritualists' National Union (SNU), in England, represents nearly four hundred Spiritualist churches and societies. According to SNU, Spiritualism is a form of philosophy and religion that holds that there is life after death, immortality and the existence of God. In 1901 the SNU adopted seven principles for the purpose of providing a definition of Spiritualism.[12] They are as follows:

1. The Fatherhood of God; a Divine energy that exists within everything.
2. The Brotherhood of Man; we are all part of the universal creative force.
3. The Communion of Spirits and the Ministry of Angels.
4. The continuous existence of the human soul.
5. Personal responsibility; free will.
6. Compensation and retribution hereafter for all the good and evil deeds done on Earth.
7. Eternal progress open to every soul.

What strikes me as most important is number four: the continuous existence of the human soul. If you believe what I'm telling you, that this is a fact, then number two, the "Brotherhood of Man," makes tremendous sense, as we are *all* in this together. If you believe in number four, then number five and number six are also strong likelihoods, as when you get to heaven there will be an opportunity to compare notes of what you did or failed to do in this life. And, I know from my own experience that number three and number seven are a reality as well. This leaves only number one, which we will leave to your imagination until one day you find yourself in heaven.

To be spiritual is to accept that we are responsible for our own actions while here on this great planet. And, it is to accept that we are responsible indirectly to each other, as our actions have the ability to affect others during our lifetime. Our race or creed or nationality does not matter.

## The Journey Continues

In this chapter you have been presented with a number of methods to assist in raising your spiritual vibration so that you may more deeply come to know who you are and why you are here. You also may better understand how a spiritual Circle may be used to build the power required for communication to those in heaven. However, the results you ultimately will experience will be proportional to the effort, energy, and focus you put into working with them.

This is an exciting time for mankind. Those in the heavenly realm are offering us this information with anticipation and hope that we may be able to bridge our two worlds closer and bring harmony to us all.

## CHAPTER 12

# HARNESSING HEAVEN

*The adventure of life is to learn. The purpose of life is to grow.*
*The nature of life is to change. The challenge of life is to overcome.*
*The essence of life is to care. The opportunity of life is to serve.*
*The secret of life is to dare. The spice of life is to befriend.*
*The beauty of life is to give. The joy of life is to love.*
—William Arthur Wood, inspirationpeak.com

The knowledge within this book has the potential to empower us in ways we can only imagine. Life is not a dry run—your time on this planet is short so make it count. It is never too late to change or to turn over a new leaf. Expanding our heart, acquiring knowledge, and becoming more of who we are is why we are here. We must seize the opportunity while we can to make a difference and be grateful for whatever we have and who we each uniquely are.

My general curiosity and desire to seek truth enabled me to find a path usually dismissed and certainly difficult to discover. There is no road map that directs "Proceed this way and you will find all the answers you seek." We persevere, pick ourselves up when we are down, and keep moving forward.

If you apply this formula to almost anything in life where you have a worthy goal, you will eventually succeed. You may even inspire others along the way, and that will be a gift to them; their joy may be a reward to you in return. Add enthusiasm and you have the magic for it to be contagious and enlist others.

Everything you do in this life counts. Every act you commit moves you forward or backward on your path. Everything you say affects others. Everything you think affects you in some way. It is all recorded in heaven in a book of life called the Akashic Records.[1]

This is your time to shine. You have the choice to set your stage in any direction you choose. You form your own reality by deciding who in this life you want to be and who the characters will be in your supporting cast. It's all up to you. Ultimately, you determine how the play will end based on what you believe. If there is any ultimate assessment from a higher power, it will be less about what is in your mind and more about what is in your heart.

As everything is energy and it has emanated from the same Source, there is a piece of this intelligence (God) in each and every one of us. This is why, even though outwardly we may all appear to be different, we are essentially the same. It is that simple. So much energy is wasted every day trying to prove otherwise.

Even the worst of us has a piece of God within. There are no discriminations from the angelic perspective; they are here to help us. It is we who label everything good or bad. When I am speaking to those on the other side of the veil, they say, "We are all *one* on this side. It's too bad you do not realize this yet on your side." This in itself indicates how out of touch we really are. We have lost our way, and it is time to find the path back.

We are all part of the same original soul, that spiritual consciousness that flows through all life on Earth. Thus, when you judge another, you judge yourself. When you cheat, lie, or steal from another, you do it to yourself. Hence, the law of karma, or the law of cause and effect, means that any act you do toward another in time returns to you. The good thing is that it applies to love as well. Any act of kindness, generosity, and compassion that emanates from your heart will also find its way back to you.

Opening your heart is the single greatest thing you can do while living your human existence. Love energy is propelled out from you in all directions and received by others near and far. As your heart opens, your vibration lightens and you become closer to the Creator. The vibration of love is strong, and it gets passed on so much farther than your immediate interaction. It can be sent huge distances by your thoughts and intentions alone. And it is felt and seen by those on the other side in the spirit world.

If for no other reason, the opening of our hearts on a massive scale may be ultimately necessary for our survival on this planet. Each of us, no matter our social standing, plays an intricate role in the tapestry of life. One heart that opens can affect many that it touches, and the process multiplies geometrically. ೞ *Connections with others are what make our life important. Love is the fabric of the universe.* ೞ An open heart, with the love it emanates, is the current that flows throughout the cosmos. It is the most powerful force that permeates all living creatures.

Mike Eruzione was the captain of the 1980 US Olympic hockey team, which upset the heavily favored Russian team to win the gold medal in Lake Placid. In an interview, he was asked how it was possible that this ragtag bunch of college boys could march into the Winter Olympics and take out a team of hockey professionals from Russia. His reply was, "We did not have as much talent as the Russians, but we really loved each other and that made the difference."[2]

## Syncing with Nature

Most of us can agree that there is a natural rhythm to the universe we live in. Look at the planets revolving around the Sun, the Moon maintaining its course around Earth, the waves breaking against the shoreline, our change of seasons, and the animal life that instinctively knows when these changes are about to occur. The rhythms and cycles are all about us; we just need to be aware of them to appreciate the magnitude of such an intricate balance occurring right in front of us each day. According to Dr. Carl Jung, "Natural life is the nourishing soil of the soul. Nature is an incomparable guide if you know how to follow her. Nature is not matter only, she is also spirit. We are in nature and think exactly like nature."[3]

There are rhythms we have long taken for granted, such as the migration of birds, whales, plants, insects, and reptiles, and even the rhythms of human beings. However, traditional planetary rhythmic templates are shifting. Consider changes we have observed in weather, sea levels, earthquakes, tsunamis, droughts, whales beaching themselves, many species becoming extinct, and broken migration patterns.

In addition, there has been a huge acceleration in our technical evolution; things are happening faster and faster. Vibrational patterns around Earth appear to be changing or shifting. The fact is that we are evolving and the world is too. Ascension is coming for this planet and its inhabitants, which means that the vibration of Earth is rising and bringing our world closer to the unseen forces of the heavenly realm. We must embrace this shift and do everything we can to prepare for it.

There may be deeper reasons for these changes occurring—perhaps an explanation beyond what our mind can comprehend—and they are affecting us for the better. Any change, though, is always met with some resistance and apprehension. This is where guidance is needed.

As evolution on the earth plane continues at a quickening pace, it is important for us to look deep within for our guiding light. This is not something separate from what we experience outside of ourself, but an integral connection we all have with the same intelligence that is responsible for the transformational processes of our planet.

For the various nations and individuals of our civilization to peacefully coexist with one another, it depends on our ability to understand that we all are one from the same Source. The sooner we learn to tap the light within, the sooner we become enlightened about who we are and why we are here. If enough people will consider this personal exploration, over time perhaps some of the insanity in the world will evolve into peace.

It cannot be just a few people who experiment with the knowledge contained in this book if we are to have a global impact. All of us need to open our minds to the reality of oneness so that our hearts can expand to embrace all of life. The same spiritual consciousness that inhabits our bodies dwells in the animals and plant life on Earth. When enough people come to the realization of their love, power, and purpose, compassion for each other will follow. It is also imperative that humanity understands that we are consciousness first and foremost occupying these human bodies. It is not the human body that creates consciousness.[4]

## Transformation

When the masses begin to understand that there is another nonphysical world existing alongside ours—just outside of our normal perception—many will want to explore and know more about it. An inspiration for living beyond blind faith will take hold. It will forever change us by bringing us closer together, with new reasons for embracing life. Death will no longer be perceived as a permanent ending point but as a change to something vital. Many hearts filled with sorrow will become lighter with joy, and great healing will unfold. Rev. Brian Robertson, a foremost Canadian medium and a leading lecturer on spiritual and psychic science and empowerment, says, "When you know there's an afterlife, you begin understanding how important this life is—that it is of value."[5]

The end result will be significant changes for the better. However, as mentioned above, change is never easy and it may take some time. The good news is that small groups of people throughout the world already are working with those in the spiritual dimension and fostering love through service and aid to those who are in need.

You can begin your own journey through removing some of the emotional layers that currently block your psychic perception. There can be events from childhood or even past lives, as others have suggested, that need releasing. Facing these painful memories is essential to inner healing. Healing emotionally and uncovering traumas from your subconscious is powerful and will greatly assist in your transformation.

As you become more sensitive, you will be able to work with those in the heavenly realm. Ultimately, our two worlds will move closer together in a partnership that is striving for similar ideas and values. Evolution will make significant progress like never before as we become unbridled and free to move forward.

Spiritualism, which was the dominant religion in the United States in the nineteenth century, may become popular once more. Although, this time it may be less about formal religious dogma and practices and more about the inner workings of what actually exists. Rather than being looked at as a religion, sharing the stage with other faiths, Spiritualism may be considered to be a belief system beyond dogma. Think of being spiritual as you would a river flowing to—and from—the Creator. The method of transportation or boat on the river is the religion or spiritual path you choose to embrace.

The reality is that we are initially a spirit born into a human body that grows old and frail and withers away. We then return once again to our normal state of being, as a spirit. There is nothing to fear, as there is more to life than just the flesh. This process is perfect.

Science is seeing a hint of this truth in quantum physics (the study and behavior of energy and matter at the molecular and subatomic levels, including the substantiated evidence that observing something can influence the physical processes taking place). String theory already shows the existence of parallel universes. Researcher Seth Lloyd has demonstrated that small atoms actually exhibit intelligence.[6] It is just a matter of time before everything ties together: science, religion, and Spiritualism.

## You Are a Big Spirit

From early in our lives people tell us how we are supposed to be. First, it is our parents, then teachers, friends, bosses, religious leaders, spouses, politicians, and, as we age, even our own children who are now adults. That is an awful lot of advice to process—and it often comes with much coaxing, in the hopes of changing us in one way or another. Since you may shed some of these learned behaviors when you cross over into heaven, why not begin removing some of those layers *now* that are not serving you? These false beliefs and automatic habits cover you like a blanket that offers protection. But you do not need any protection, as there is a power within you bigger than anything you have ever imagined—your spirit, soul, or divine essence.

Bestselling author and prominent alternative-medicine advocate Deepak Chopra, in *The Seven Spiritual Laws of Success*, counsels us to pursue this power: "Discover your divinity, find your unique talent, serve humanity with it, and you can generate all the wealth you want."[7] Look within your own heart to begin unlocking your power. Even if you think your heart is already open, there is still more room for expansion. Don't allow fear to hold you back, as it may trickle into your thinking if you permit it.

As you open your heart, this draws you closer to the Creator, Source, God—whatever term works best for you. This open-heartedness can bring you clarity and truth, and begin to reveal your reason for being here. Undoubtedly, it will bring you more peace and more fulfilling relationships.

Have strength if your own heart is open while those of others around you are closed. You are not weak; it takes great fortitude and conviction to hold your ground in a gathering storm. Hold your head high, knowing you are living the life you have intended. Sometimes, as a result of your speaking your truth, friends may fall away, but do not be concerned—in time, others will notice your authenticity and steadfastness of purpose and seek you out.

Live your life as if there is no second chance. Approach your interests with passion and set an example for others to follow. This will provide you with a lightness of being, knowing you are giving all you can to make a difference in the world.

In an effort to assist you in living your life to its fullest, I would like to share with you an interesting piece on what people were thinking as they approached the end of their lifetime. According to author Bronnie Ware,[8] the top five things people regretted before dying are:

1. I wish I'd had the courage to live a life true to myself.
2. I wish I hadn't worked so hard.
3. I wish I'd had the courage to express my feelings.
4. I wish I had stayed in touch with my friends.
5. I wish that I had let myself be happier.

Divine guidance always says it is essential to serve others and be of assistance whenever possible. Service is a great contribution to bestow on people, and we can help those who are less fortunate and those in need. As we assist others, we are lifted in the process. The human chain of life is only as strong as its weakest link. Society sometimes fails to see this small but important point. As we strengthen the weak links, it helps us all to move farther along in our evolutionary progress. As heavyweight-boxing champion Muhammad Ali once said, "Service to others is the rent you pay for your room here on Earth."[9]

For some, there is a feeling or distinction we experience that works against one of the basic principles of the universe. It is that we often feel different from others, which leads us to falsely believe we are separate from them. Yes, Spirit expresses its creativity by making us all unique individuals; this is what makes life so rich and full. However, it does not mean that we are not all part of the larger whole. We are all united in this wonderful experience to physically express ourselves and emotionally experience the ups and downs life brings us. It is a joy to discover our spiritual gifts, and this must not be taken for granted.

What you want from life, what it gives you, and how you react to the differences with others as well as the similarities will greatly define your experience during your brief time here. Your true essence is eternal; your current existence is but a brief chapter in the everlasting timeline, and you are the author. You have the freedom to create the story.

## *You Were Born to Rise*

We all must understand that we are not alone, ever. The truth that has been expressed many times in this book is that *all life* emanates from Spirit, or the Creator, God, the Maker—whatever term works for you—and will forever share that innate connection. This is the reality, and it is time for mainstream thinking to reach this clarity. Understanding this basic premise is one way civilization will be able to safely move itself forward. We must stop destroying each other as well as the environment and the planet needed to support us.

You do not need to be a sociologist to see a lack of belief by many for existence beyond what we can see. Turning on world news each night gives a huge dose of fear-based data about death, showing how some in power terrorize and control the weak with a fear of loss. We have a long way to evolve as a civilization.

Progress with technology provide conveniences and efficiencies, but they do not necessarily help us grow spiritually. This is a personal matter that each of us needs to consider individually and in our own way. Technology can be a double-edged sword: it has the ability to make the world a smaller place as we interact with people around the world via social media. However, we can also get too caught up in its allure and sometimes fail to notice what is going on around us.

When I wrote this material with my spirit guides, I was leaving my comfort zone. My thoughts were telling me it was risky and that people would judge me from all sides. My heart said to go ahead and make a difference in others' lives—that this information was just too important to sweep under the rug. It could help people begin to understand the power they possess, perhaps help heal some individuals, and maybe bring us closer together as we realize we are more similar than different.

Where you are today is the sum of all your past decisions. If you change your thinking, you can change your life. If you can listen to your heart, you have a compass for directing you on your course. You may open a world of new possibilities going forward without giving up anything you already have accomplished.

Ask yourself these questions: Do I feel peace within myself? Is there a still, small voice whispering within me or a feeling in my gut to which I am listening? Have I made time for reflection on my choices? How many other lives have I positively affected? Have I helped anyone in need?

When you help someone, if even only for a moment, you assist in your personal evolution as well. When you show compassion for another human being, your heart expands. Like any other muscle in your body, it becomes stronger over time.

If there were a basic prescription I could give you for how to live while on this planet, it would be "Love yourself; love others." Your time here is brief, so it is critical to make it count. You already have the gift of intuition and perhaps the spiritual abilities of seeing, hearing, feeling, and/or knowing. You only need to set your intention and begin your journey to reap the rewards. You are responsible for yourself and your progression—no one else can do this for you.

Following are some simple thoughts to live by that I have learned along my own personal path:

1. Know that you are never alone.
2. Forgive yourself and everyone else.
3. Learn from your past—do not dwell on it. Your future is comprised of the sum total of your present moments.
4. Believe that you are lovable, and love others without expectation.
5. Accept that you are here for a purpose and that all is well.

We were put here to learn, to expand ourselves in so many ways, to radiate, to help others, and to teach. As we ultimately learn these ways of living, war, famine, oppression, and hate will be replaced with a higher calling. Each of us needs to begin, one by one, opening up to our inner light, our soul, to discover the larger purpose for our existence. Using some of the techniques from chapter 11 will enable you to start this process. Then you will discover there is no turning back.

Like in the movie *The Matrix*, if you choose not to discover the spiritual part of yourself, the story ends; you wake up in your bed and believe whatever you want to believe. However, if you choose to explore and follow the words shared within these pages, you go to "wonderland" and discover how deep the rabbit hole goes.

I would like to close this journey with you with a profound quote by Silver Birch, a spirit guide channeled by Spiritualist Maurice Barbanell:

> The first step is for the world to begin healing. Until the people of the world realize they are souls and not physical bodies, they will continue going through life indifferent to reality—chasing illusions. It is only when they become aware of their real selves, their spiritual natures, that they come face to face with reality. To find yourself is an object of all Earthly life, because once you find yourself you will then, if you are wise, proceed to develop that divinity which lies within you.[10]

It takes only one small light to illuminate a dark room. We will all move forward one person at a time, and yet all of our lights together can illuminate our planet and, ultimately, the entire universe, with both its physical and spiritual dimensions.

Our friends in heaven are ready and willing to assist us on

our journey; all we have to do is open to this cocreative possibility—harness their wisdom and guidance—and they will happily join us. A partnership awaits us all. It is now time to turn your light on; ascension is right in front of you. What are you waiting for?

# Acknowledgments

There are many who helped put this project together and others who enabled me to find the courage and wisdom to begin writing and working with the heavenly realm. Those who provided support for *Harnessing Heaven* fall into five distinct categories.

My heartfelt thanks goes to:

The "book-production experts" who worked tirelessly to bring this book to its highest potential: Maggie Lichtenberg, Barbara Doern Drew, Lori Martinsek, Dr. Janet Cunningham, Peter Bowerman, Hobie Hobart, Kathi Dunn, and Dorie McClelland.

The "consultants who sprinkled their wisdom" about the style and flow of the material: Michael Bettencourt, Debra Herman, Gail Lionetti, Robyn Fatooh, and Louise Mickelson.

The "spiritual lights" who saw my path even when I did not: Warfield Mosse Jr., Nini Grace, Audrey Willey, Lee Ann La Rocca, and Susan Conner.

"Those who helped build my wings" (discovery is a never ending process): Trish Woods, Stephanie Ezzat, Jeannie Pacheco, Janet Nohavic, Lee Van Zyl, Maria Kramer, Nancy Russell, Simon James, Brian Robertson, Colin Bates, and Steven Upton, as well as my companions in the spiritual dimension, whose unbounded support enabled me to find the inspiration, strength, and courage to fill the words on these pages.

The "Big Spirit"—God, the Creator—who gave me a second

chance to live my life so that I can be in service to others and bring harmony to this remarkable world we all share.

Finally, I would like to thank my family: my wife, Heather, for her love and inspiration, along with the freedom for me to explore a part of reality hidden from her view. And my sons, Darin and Brandon, who remind me each day how blessed I am as a father to witness the miracle of creation wrapped in innocence that only a child brings into this world.

APPENDIX A

# Chakra Energy Centers

Energy can flow through us, just as it moves throughout the universe. The human body has chakras, receptors that are designed to channel this energy (*prana*) within us. Although there are many energy receptors, there are seven main chakras that process this energy flow for our well-being.

The following descriptions for each chakra cite its location in the body, associated anatomy and indicate how it relates to our thoughts, feelings, emotions, and ways of being. As we change our behaviors, this changes our energy, our chakras, and the auric field that surrounds us. If we have an unresolved personal issue, the particular related chakra may not function properly. In addition, there are specific musical notes that correspond to each chakra, and using this sound can help rebalance the energy center.

**First, or "root," chakra**: Base of the spine, gonads, and intestines. Relates to survival in society, energy for life, stability, security, strength, trust, and being grounded. Musical note "C."

**Second, or "sacral," chakra**: Lower abdomen, pelvis, kidney and bodily fluids. Accepting of others, feelings, creativity, desire, passion, sexuality, emotion, guilt, pleasure, and abundance. Musical note "D."

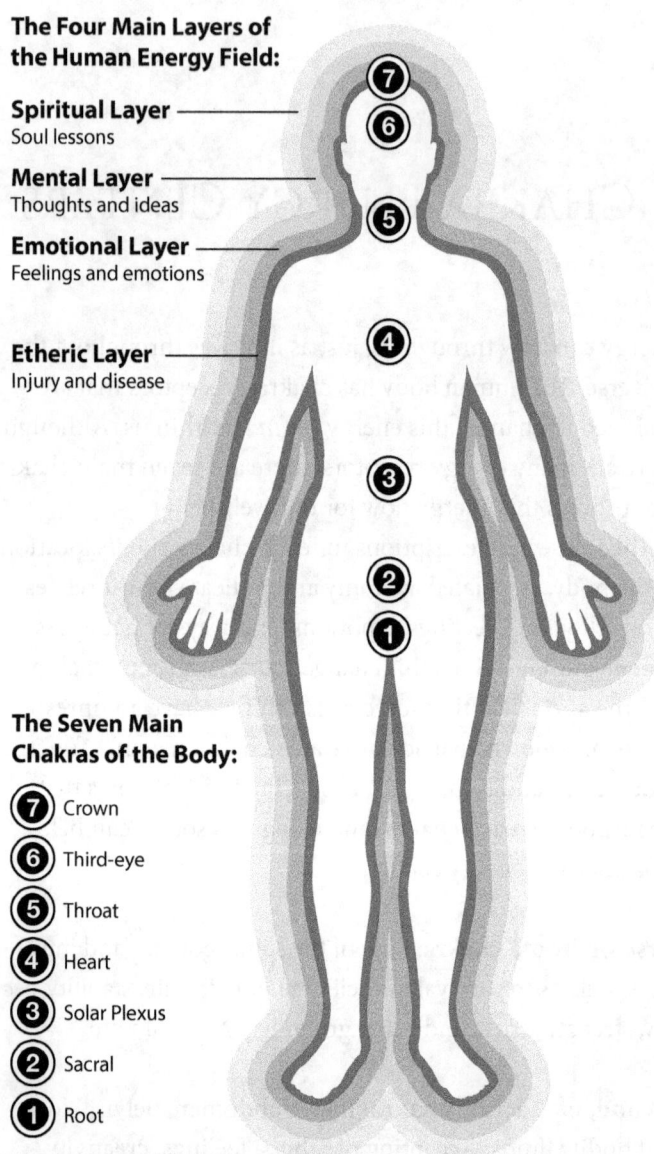

*Note*: While there are more than four energy layers in the human aura and additional chakras of the body, this diagram illustrates the main themes.

*Appendix A*

**Third chakra**: Solar plexus, digestive and nervous system. Self-acceptance, self-worth, self-esteem, confidence; feelings of anger, joy, and fear; a sense of being in control, ego, personal power. Musical note "E."

**Fourth chakra**: Thymus, heart, and lungs. Love, peace, unity, empathy, forgiveness, compassion for all living things. Musical note "F."

**Fifth chakra**: Thyroid, throat, voice and neck. Expression, communication, truthfulness, will power, integrity. Musical note "G."

**Sixth, or "third eye," chakra**: Pituitary gland, sinus and eyes. Seeing clearly, wisdom, imagination, intuition, inspiration, discernment, knowing, perception. Musical note "A."

**Seventh, or "crown," chakra**: Pineal gland, brain and top of the head. Seeking God or spirituality, connectedness, one with creation, understanding. Musical note "B."

APPENDIX B

# Evaluating Your Energy Centers to Raise Your Vibration

Our thought patterns and ultimately our emotions can raise us up or bring us down. As discussed in chapter 5, there can be emotional residue that finds its way into the energy centers throughout the human body—in essence, energy that takes physical form inside ourselves that can be released or withheld.

Releasing and clearing the residue from our own chakras helps to power us so we may bridge the gap between the two worlds of the physical and the unseen. It likely took a long time to accumulate blockages in your own chakras, so please be patient, as it may take some time for you to clear.

The "Personal Evaluation Chart" that follows is designed to assist you in recognizing which chakras may need your attention. There is no correct answer, only one that presently reflects your state of being. Ideally, one would aspire to have a higher average number in the top half of the chart ("Balance of Male/Female Traits") and a lower average number in the bottom half ("Positive/Negative Creative Forces"). When you have completed this exercise, you may be surprised by your own behavior patterns and which chakras are working to their capacity and which need clearing work.

*Appendix B*

# INSTRUCTIONS FOR PERSONAL EVALUATION CHART

The Personal Evaluation Chart is meant to help you look at the balance of masculine and feminine traits within you. It also scores your positive and negative expressions of the Creative Forces within each of the chakra/gland centers by having you assign number values to them.

There is a column for each of the chakra-gland combinations. The top half of the column lists positive attributes of that center, while the bottom half represents the negative expression.

1. Use the legend below to score yourself on each of the attributes:

   1 = Never; 2 = Seldom; 3 = Occasionally;
   4 = Frequently; 5 = Habitually; 6 = Always

2. Total the numbers at the top of the column (Positive Attributes) and then divide by 10. You should get an answer from 1 to 6 that tells you how balanced your masculine and feminine energies are. **The higher the number the better.**

3. Now total the numbers at the bottom of the column (Negative Attributes) and then divide by 10. Again you should get an answer from 1 to 6 that indicates if you are using the Creative Forces of this center in a positive or negative way. **The lower the number the better.**

4. Example: Column IV Heart/Thymus—top half

   | Attribute | Score |
   |---|---|
   | Thoughtful of others | 4 |
   | Magnifies virtues | 2 |
   | Appreciative | 4 |
   | Friendly | 5 |
   | Sincere | 6 |
   | Generous | 3 |
   | Punctual | 6 |
   | Sense of humor | 6 |
   | Accepts criticism | 4 |
   | Sympathetic | 4 |

   Total = 44 divide by 10 = 4.4

5. **Example: Column IV—bottom half**

   | Attribute | Score |
   |---|---|
   | Feels Inadequate | 2 |
   | Overly sentimental | 2 |
   | Self-centered | 3 |
   | Cynical | 2 |
   | Withdraws | 4 |
   | Self-conscious | 5 |
   | Does not share | 5 |
   | Late | 1 |
   | Blames others | 2 |
   | Self-pity | 1 |

   Total = 27 divide by 10 = 2.7

   Average for this center is a little less than occasionally 2.7. The high scores of 4 and the 5s might indicate that this chakra is somewhat closed. (You can make your own interpretations.)

6. Do the same for each column. After you have completed calculating the seven columns, take a look at each of the totals, paying particular attention to the high scores in the bottom columns. Those high scores indicate unconscious patterns that are impairing the flow of a higher level of vibrational energy in that center. Begin to change your automatic responses to situations from the negative to the positive by focusing on the ideal of LOVE when that trait is triggered. The following exercise can help you begin this process of transformation.

**Exercise: Negative Attitude Clearing**

1. Go back to Column I—the Root Chakra/Gonads. Select the negative trait from the bottom of the column that had the highest score. If there are several with the same score, pick the one that you feel more emotion about than the others.

2. Allow a thought or the remembrance of a situation in which you exhibited this trait to come to mind.

3. Now begin to change it by thinking the opposite—the positive—of that trait. Imagine yourself in that remem-

*Appendix B*

bered situation only this time embodying the positive aspect. Experience how that feels. If there is anyone else involved, see how that person responds differently. Understand the new emotion of this. As you do, affirm that you desire to transform that old, negative attitude into the new positive one.

4. Do the same procedure for each of the seven column/energy centers.

5. When you are done, you may want to journal your thoughts and experiences.

6. The more you do this exercise, the more you will begin to change those unconscious patterns that have built up over the ages. These are the persistent ones that require your commitment to transform.

7. Pay attention to how your reality changes as you begin to exhibit these positive traits in your daily life now.

This chart is included on the next pages courtesy of the A.R.E. electronic course, "Vibrations at Atlantic University."

*Harnessing Heaven*

# A PERSONAL EVALUATION CHART

Beside each positive/negative expression of the Creative Force, through the chakra/gland, put the appropriate number opposite each expression, add each column (top section, then bottom), and divide by 10 for an average.

LEGEND:  1 = Never     3 = Occasionally   5 = Habitually
         2 = Seldom    4 = Frequently     6 = Always

| I Root/ Gonads | II Sacral/ Lyden | III Solar Plexus/ Adrenals | IV Heart/ Thymus |
|---|---|---|---|
| **Balance of Male-Female Traits** | | | |
| Helpful | Justice | Takes initiative | Thoughtful of others |
| Protective | Courteous | Persistent | Magnifies virtues |
| Hard worker | Consistent | Enthusiastic | Appreciative |
| Strong, healthy | Resolute | Participates | Friendly |
| Wholesome | Mercy | Takes responsibility | Sincere |
| Creative in arts | Gentle | Peacemaker | Generous |
| Controls appetites | Gracious | Courage | Punctual |
| Loves others | Orderly | Patient | Sense of humor |
| Meditates daily | Intuitive | Strives to improve | Accepts criticism |
| Has hobbies | Patient | Controls temper | Sympathetic |
| **Positive/Negative Creative Forces** (add the appropriate number from above legend) | | | |
| Forces | Doubt | Destructive | Feels inadequate |
| Abuses | Shows off, ostentation | Holds back | Overly sentimental |
| Overdoes or lazy | Foolhardy | Easily discouraged | Self-centered |
| Prudish or vulgar | Irresponsible | "Wet blanket" | Cynical |
| Unimaginative | Cynical | Domineering | Withdrawn |
| Materialistic | Inflexible | Timid, fearful | Self-conscious |
| Indulges appetites | Unrealistic | Easily frustrated | Does not share |
| Does not meditate | Shy, withdrawn | Anger | Late |
| Coarse language | Gullible | Uncontrolled temper | Blames others |
| "Sweet tooth" | Imbalance of masculine/ feminine | Hate | Self-pity |

## Appendix B

**LEGEND:**    1 = Never    3 = Occasionally    5 = Habitually
                  2 = Seldom    4 = Frequently     6 = Always

| V Throat/ Thyroid | VI Third-Eye/ Pineal | VII Crown/ Pituitary |
|---|---|---|
| Controls choices | Intelligent | Sense of oneness |
| Consistent | Alert | Inspires others |
| Obedient | Seeking | Spiritual humility |
| Cooperative | Open-minded | Reverent |
| Self-disciplined | Asks questions | General control |
| Stands by ideals | Evaluates | Dedicated |
| Peace of mind | Knows self | Gives God "credit" |
| Communicates well | Aware of conscience | Encourages others |
| Subject to God's will | Reasonable | Understanding |
| Open to suggestions | Logical | Healing ability |

**Positive/Negative Creative Forces** (add the appropriate number from above legend)

| | | |
|---|---|---|
| Fluctuates | Slow to learn | No sense of oneness |
| Rebellious | Vague | Deflates others |
| Stubborn | Narrow-minded | Tempts others |
| Self-willed | Gullible | Spiritual pride |
| Can't communicate | Rationalizes | No general control |
| Careless | Unthinking | Self-righteous |
| Inattentive | Does not know self | Spiritually arrogant |
| Does not apply | No conscience | Idealistically impractical |
| Closed to suggestion | Unreasonable | Lack of vision |
| Indecisive | Illogical | No sense of relation to group |

APPENDIX C

# Resources for Learning about Energy and Spirituality

There are many authors with published information who can help provide some perspective on energy, auras, psychic development, spiritual influences, and personal development. Some authors are mentioned in this book; others can easily be found through an Internet search. Use discernment when seeking out information and attending metaphysical classes.

*Reading*

Barbara Brennan, *Hands of Light: A Guide to Healing Through the Human Energy Field*
Rosalyn L. Bruyere, *Wheels of Light: Chakras, Auras, and the Healing Energy of the Body*
Edgar Cayce, *Beyond Death: Visions of the Other Side*
Edgar Cayce, *Reincarnation and Karma*
Kim Chestney, *The Psychic Workshop: A Complete Program for Fulfilling Your Spiritual Potential*
Deepak Chopra, *The Seven Spiritual Laws of Success: A Practical Guide to the Fulfillment of Your Dreams*
Susan Collins, *Dowsing That Works: Use a Protocol to Get Results*

## Appendix C

Cyndi Dale, *New Chakra Healing: Activate Your 32 Energy Centers*

Cyndi Dale, *The Subtle Body: An Encyclopedia of Your Energetic Anatomy*

Wayne Dyer, *The Power of Intention: Learning to Co-create Your World Your Way*

Masaru Emoto, *Love Thyself: The Message from Water III*

B. Ernest Frejer, *The Edgar Cayce Companion: A Comprehensive Treatise of the Edgar Cayce Readings*

Diane Goldner, *How People Heal: Exploring the Scientific Basis of Subtle Energy in Healing*

David R. Hawkins, *Power vs. Force: The Hidden Determinants of Human Behavior*

David R. Hawkins, *Transcending the Levels of Consciousness: The Stairway to Enlightenment*

Louise L. Hay, *Heal Your Body: The Mental Causes for Physical Illness and the Metaphysical Way to Overcome Them*

Ernest Holmes and Willis Kinnear, *Thoughts Are Things*

Elaine Hruska, *When Illness Strikes: Let Edgar Cayce Help You Manifest Your Healing Response*

Dennis Merritt Jones, *The Art of Being: 101 Ways to Practice Purpose in Your Life*

Raymond A. Moody, Jr., *Life After Life: The Investigation of a Phenomenon—Survival of Bodily Death*

Caroline Myss, *Anatomy of the Spirit: The Seven Stages of Power and Healing*

Tony Ortzen, *More Philosophy of Silver Birch: Teachings from the Silver Birch Series*

Jane Roberts, *Seth Speaks: The Eternal Validity of the Soul*

Jane Roberts, *The Unknown Reality: Volume One*

M. Scott Peck, *The Road Less Traveled: A New Psychology of Love, Traditional Values and Spiritual Growth*

Paul Selig, *I Am the Word: A Guide to the Consciousness of Man's Self in a Transitioning Time*

Susan G. Shumsky, *Exploring Auras: Cleansing and Strengthening Your Energy Field*

Stevan J. Thayer and Linda Sue Nathanson, *Interview with an Angel*

James Van Praagh, *Reaching to Heaven: A Spiritual Journey Through Life and Death*

James Van Praagh, *Unfinished Business: What the Dead Can Teach Us About Life*

Ambika Wauters, *The Book of Chakras: Discover the Hidden Forces Within You*

Brian Weiss, *Many Lives, Many Masters: The True Story of a Prominent Psychiatrist, His Young Patient, and the Past-Life Therapy That Changed Both Their Lives*

White Eagle, *Spiritual Unfoldment I: How to Discover the Invisible Worlds and Find the Source of Healing*

Marianne Williamson, *A Return to Love: Reflections on the Principles of a Course in Miracles*

Gary Zukav, *The Seat of the Soul*

*Education and Classes*

A.R.E. of Virginia: 215 67th Street, Virginia Beach, VA 23451; www.edgarcayce.org; 800-333-4499

A.R.E. of New York City: 241 West 30th Street #102, NY, NY 10001; www.edgarcaycenyc.org; 212-691-7690

Arthur Findlay College (England): Stansted Hall, Stansted Mountfitchet, Essex, United Kingdom CM24 8UD; www.arthurfindlaycollege.org; tel. 01279813636

*Appendix C*

*Other Resources*

American Society of Dowsers (ASD): 184 Brainerd Street, PO Box 24, Danville, VT 05828; www.dowsers.org; 802-684-3417

Spiritual Development Circles: www.spiritualistresources.com (offers a partial listing of development circles in some parts of the world)

*Sound for Meditation and Balancing*

Hemi-Sync: www.hemi-sync.com; 434-263-8692
The Relaxation Company: www.therelaxationcompany.com
Sounds True: www.soundstrue.com; 800-333-9185

# Chapter Notes

*Chapter 1*
1. Edgar Cayce's A.R.E., Association for Research and Enlightenment, 215 67th Street, Virginia Beach, VA 23451, www.edgarcayce.org.
2. B. Ernest Frejer, *The Edgar Cayce Companion: A Comprehensive Treatise of the Edgar Cayce Readings* (Virginia Beach, VA: A.R.E. Press, 1995).
3. Ibid.

*Chapter 2*
1. Brian L. Weiss, MD, *Through Time into Healing* (New York: Simon & Schuster, 1992).
2. Eckhart Tolle, *The Power of Now* (Novato, CA: New World Library, 2004).
3. Albert Einstein, "Albert Einstein Quotes," Brainy Quote, http://brainyquote.com/quotes/quotes/a/alberteins145949.html.

*Chapter 4*
1. Raymond A. Moody, Jr., MD, *Life After Life: The Investigation of a Phenomenon—Survival of Bodily Death* (New York, NY: Harper Collins Publishers, Inc., 2008).
2. David McKinley, "Brian Tracy's Quote of the Day," Brian Tracy Quotes, briantracy.com.
3. Deut. 6:4–9; Mark 12:28–30.
4. Edwin Hubble, "A Relation Between Distance and Radial Velocity Among Extra-Galactic Nebulae," *Proceedings of the National Academy of Sciences of the United States of America* 15, no. 3 (1929), 168–173.
5. Dr. Wayne Dyer, "Wayne Dyer Quotes," http://izquotes.com/author/wayne-dyer.
6. Francois-Marie Arouet (Voltaire), "Voltaire Quotes," Brainy Quote, http://brainyquote.com/quotes/quotes/v/voltaire132884.html.
7. Anais Nin, "Anais Nin Quotes," Brainy Quote, http://brainyquote.com/quotes/quotes/a/anaisin107089html.
8. Carl Young, MD, *The Earth Has a Soul* (Berkeley, CA: North Atlantic Books, 2008).

## Chapter 5

1. Semyon and Valentina Kirilian, "Photography and Visual Observation by Means of High Frequency Currents," *Russian Journal of Scientific and Applied Photography*, 1961. Sheila Ostrander and Lynn Schroeder, *Psychic Discoveries Behind the Iron Curtain* (Englewood Cliffs, NJ: Prentice Hall, 1970).
2. Cyndi Dale, *New Chakra Healing* (Woodbury, MN: Llewellyn Publications, 1996).
3. Katherine Kam and Louise Chang, MD, "How Anger Hurts Your Heart," *Web MD Magazine* (2009).
4. Louise L. Hay, *Heal Your Body* (Carlsbad, CA: Hay House, Inc., 1988), 2.
5. White Eagle, *Spiritual Unfoldment I* (Hampshire, England: The White Eagle Publishing Trust, 2006).
6. Edgar Cayce, "Edgar Cayce Reading 2812-1," Edgar Cayce's A.R.E., Association for Research and Enlightenment, 215 67th Street, Virginia Beach, VA 23451, www.edgarcayce.org.
7. Ernest Holmes and Willis Kinnear, *Thoughts Are Things* (Deerfield Beach, FL: Health Communications Inc., 1967).
8. Dale, *New Chakra Healing*.
9. Stevan J. Thayer, *Integrated Energy Therapy* (Woodstock, NY: The Center of Being, 1996).
10. Barbara Ann Brennan, *Hands of Light: A Guide to Healing Through the Human Energy Field* (New York: Bantam Books, 1988).
11. Dale, *New Chakra Healing*.
12. Brennan, *Hands of Light*.
13. Carl G. Jung, MD, *The Earth Has a Soul* (Berkeley, CA: North Atlantic Books, 2008).
14. Diane Goldner, *How People Heal* (Charlottesville, VA: Hampton Roads Publishing Co., 1999).
15. Buddha, "Buddha Quotes," Brainy Quote, https://brainyquote.com/quotes/quotes/b/buddha121206html.
16. Daily Om—Nurturing Mind Body & Spirit: "Flying Home Free of Gravity," April 27, 2007, dailyom.com.
17. Bruce Lee, Wikiquote, https://en.wikiquote.org/wiki/Bruce_lee.
18. Edgar Cayce, "Edgar Cayce Reading 3253-2," Edgar Cayce's A.R.E., Association for Research and Enlightenment, 215 67th Street, Virginia Beach, VA 23451, www.edgarcayce.org.

## Chapter 6

1. Columbia University Earth Institute: Lamont-Doherty Earth Observatory, 2013.
2. *The Matrix*, written and directed by the Wachowski Brothers, produced by Joel Silver (Warner Bros. Pictures, 1999).
3. Ernest Holmes, *The Essential Ernest Holmes*, ed. Jesse Jennings (New York: Jeremy P. Tarcher/Putnam, 2002), 172.
4. Stephen A. Ross and Randolph W. Chesterfield, *Fundamentals of Corporate Finance* (New York: McGraw-Hill Companies, 2003).
5. Albert Einstein, "Albert Einstein Quotes," Brainy Quote, https://brainyquote.com/quotes/quotes/a/alberteins121993.html.

## Chapter 7

1. Jane Roberts, *Seth Speaks* (New York: Bantam Books, 1972).
2. Leonard Jacobson, "Jacobson Quotes," https://www.azquotes.com/authors/l/leonardjacobson.
3. Kuan Yin, "Inspirational Quotes," Android, https://play.google.com/store/apps/details?id=com.rantaz.sgquoteslife&hl=en.
4. White Eagle, *Spiritual Unfoldment I* (Hampshire, England: The White Eagle Publishing Trust, 2006).
5. *Wikipedia*, s.v. "Ring of Fire," http://en.wikipedia.org/wiki/Ring_of_Fire. Source further explored: Matt Rosenberg, "Pacific Ring of Fire," Ring of Fire—Home to Earthquakes and Volcanoes of the Earth, June 14, 2010, http://geography.about.com/cs/earthquakes/a/ringoffire.htm.
6. Ibid.
7. Gordon Michael Scallion, *Intuitive Flash* (West Chesterfield, NH: Matrix Institute, 2011).
8. Tony Phillips, cited in *Modern Survival Blog*: "Polar Shift and Earthquakes Today," blog entry by Ken Jorgustin, October 8, 2010.
9. Guy Adams, "Adjust your compass now: the north pole is migrating to Russia," *The Independent*, March 6, 2011, http://www.independent.co.uk/news/science/adjust-your-compass-now-the-north-pole-is-migrating-to-russia-2233610.html.

## Chapter 8

1. Ralph Waldo Emerson, "Ralph Waldo Emerson Quotes," Brainy Quote, www.brainyquote.com/quotes/quotes/r/ralphwaldo151956.html.
2. Colleen Sexton, *J. K. Rowling (A&E Biography)*, (A&E Television Networks, 2010).
3. Michael Jordan, "Brian Tracy's Quote of the Day," Brian Tracy Quotes, briantracy.com.
4. Edgar Cayce, Edgar Cayce's A.R.E., Association for Research and Enlightenment, 215 67th Street, Virginia Beach, VA 23451. www.edgarcayce.org.
5. Carl G. Jung, MD, *The Earth Has a Soul* (Berkeley, CA: North Atlantic Books, 2008).
6. *The Beatles Anthology*, film produced by L. Wolff (Apple Corps Limited, 1995).
7. Betty J. Eddie, *Embraced by the Light: The Most Profound and Complete Near-Death Experience Ever* (New York: Bantam Books, 1994).

## Chapter 9

1. Brian L. Weiss, MD, *Through Time into Healing* (New York: Simon & Schuster, 1992).
2. Albert Einstein, *Einstein on Cosmic Religion and Other Opinions and Aphorisms* (New York: Dover Publications, 1931; rerelease 2009).
3. Esther and Jerry Hicks, *The Law of Attraction: The Basics of the Teachings of Abraham* (Hay House, Inc., 2006), www.hayhouse.com.

## Chapter 10

1. Zig Ziglar, "Zig Ziglar Quotes," www.quoteswise.com/zig-ziglar-quotes-4.html.
2. Joel Osteen, Joel Osteen Ministries, http://www.facebook.com/Joelosteen/posts/10151763762375227.
3. Matt. 7:7, World English Bible, https://ebible.org/web/.
4. Edgar Cayce, Edgar Cayce's A.R.E on Spiritual Growth, www.edgarcayce.org/are/spiritualGrowth.aspx.
5. Carl G. Jung, MD, *The Earth Has a Soul* (Berkeley, CA: North Atlantic Books, 2008).
6. Tony Robbins, "Quotes by Tony Robbins," www.goodreads.com/quotes/165556-the-past-does-not-equal-the-future.

Notes to Chapters 10–11

7. Wayne W. Dyer, https://www.facebook.com/drwaynedyer/posts/10150996736971030.
8. Denis Waitley, "Denis Waitley Quotes," Brainy Quote, www.brainyquote.com/quotes/quotes/d/deniswaitl146905.html.
9. Buddha, "Buddha Quotes," Brainy Quote, www.brainyquote.com/quotes/quotes/b/buddha121206.html.
10. *Gladiator*, written by David Franzoni, directed by Ridley Scott, produced by Douglas Wick, David Franzoni, and Branko Lustig (Dream Works Pictures and Universal Pictures, 2000).
11. Rudolf Steiner, *Atlantis and Lemuria* (London: Theosophical Publishing Society, 1911; United States: Dr. Weller Van Hook, copyright 1911).
12. Nickelback, vocal performance of "If Today Was Your Last Day," by Chad Kroeger, on *Dark Horse*, produced by Robert John "Mutt" Lange and Joey Moi (2008).

*Chapter 11*

1. White Eagle, *Spiritual Unfoldment I* (Hampshire, England: The White Eagle Publishing Trust, 2006).
2. Bishop T.D. Jakes, "T.D. Jakes," www.goodreads.com/quotes/636989-if-you-can-t-figure-out-your-purpose-figure-out-your-passion.
3. Esther and Jerry Hicks, *Law of Attraction Journal: The Teachings of Abraham*, (Abraham-Hicks Publications, 2010).
4. Elaine K. Jackson, *Awakening to Gratitude: Create a New Reality of Freedom and Abundance* (Fairfax, CA: The Gratitude Power Foundation, 2010).
5. Edgar Cayce, "Reading 1424-2," Edgar Cayce's A.R.E., Association for Research and Enlightenment, 215 67th Street, Virginia Beach, VA 23451, www.edgarcayce.org.
6. Tatjana-Mihaela, "How Sound Creates Universe and Our Material Reality," *HubPages*, February 24, 2009, http://tatjana-mihaela.hubpages.com/hub/power-of-sound.
7. Carol J. Wyche, "Yoga As Energy Healing: Unknotting a tangle is always easier if you work both ends," *Pathfinder*, 2012, http://www.pathfindertohealth.com/articles/yoga_energy_healing.htm.
8. Walt Woods, *Letter to Robin: A Mini-Course in Pendulum Dowsing* (St. Johnsbury, VT: The American Society of Dowsers, March 2001).

9. Susan Collins, *Dowsing That Works: Use a Protocal to Get Results* (King City, Ontario: Puka Ha/Golden Crow, 2008).
10. The Spiritualists' National Union, Stansted Hall, Standsted, Essex, UK CM24 8UD, http://www.snu.org.uk/spiritualism/religion.
11. Nettie Coburn Maynard, *Nettie Coburn Maynard Trance Medium* (Great Britain: SDU Publications, 2009).
12. The Spiritualists' National Union, Stansted Hall, Standsted, Essex, UK CM24 8UD, http://www.snu.org.uk/spiritualism/principles.

### Chapter 12

1. Kevin Todeschi, *Edgar Cayce on the Akashic Records* (Virginia Beach, VA: A.R.E. Press, 1998).
2. Mike Eruzione, USA Men's Hockey 1980 Olympics, originally reported by ABC Television Network, 1980. Rebroadcast by HBO Sports: *Do You Believe in Miracles: The Story of the 1980 U.S. Hockey Team* (New York: HBO Home Video, 2001).
3. Carl G. Jung, MD, *The Earth Has a Soul* (Berkeley, CA: North Atlantic Books, 2008).
4. Jane Roberts, *Seth Speaks* (New York: Bantam Books, 1972).
5. As quoted with permission from a conversation in 2014 in New Jersey with teacher and speaker Rev. Brian Robertson, who resides in Victoria, British Columbia, Canada.
6. Seth Lloyd, *Programming the Universe: A Quantum Computer Scientist Takes on the Cosmos* (New York: Vintage Books, Random House, 2007).
7. Deepak Chopra, *The Seven Spiritual Laws of Success* (San Rafael, CA: New World Library, 1994), 101.
8. Bronnie Ware, *The Top Five Regrets of the Dying: A Life Transformed by the Dearly Departing* (Hay House, Inc.: www.Hayhouse.com, 2012).
9. Muhammad Ali, "Muhammad Ali Quotes," Brainy Quote, www.brainyquote.com/quotes/quotes/m/muhammadel136676.html.
10. Silver Birch, Silver Birch's teachings through Maurice Barbanell, answers to questions (The Spiritual Truth Foundation, www.Silverbirchpublishing.co.uk).

# About the Author

Clifford Michaels works in New York City as an investment adviser and financial planner. His thirty years on Wall Street led him to become the president of the Financial Planning Association of New York. He has appeared on CNN, CNBC, and PBS 13, and has contributed to articles that have appeared in *Money Magazine*, *Smart Money*, *Newsday*, the *Wall Street Digest*, *Bloomberg Business*, and the *Dow Jones Newswire*. Clifford has taught financial topics as adult education at St. John's University and at Baruch College. He holds a BS from Syracuse University and an MBA from the University of Pittsburgh.

With a foot in two worlds, so to speak, Clifford can help transmit light—either energy for healing or words for communication—from the other side, bringing comfort and healing to others. His desire is to raise humanity's awareness to the true existence of who they are, which will aid in bringing peace among all people. In addition to his spiritual writing, he also teaches metaphysics.

Clifford can be reached at
Cliffordmichaels@Harnessingheaven.com
or through his website,
www.HarnessingHeaven.com.

www.ingramcontent.com/pod-product-compliance
Lightning Source LLC
Chambersburg PA
CBHW070559300426
44113CB00010B/1317